"Unstoppable is the perfect word to capture the essence of Betsy. She generously shares her inspiring stories of life and business. Her unstoppable recipe is filled with great ingredients for any journey!"

-*Kathleen Wood*
Founder of Kathleen Wood Partners
Growth Strategist, Motivational Speaker and Author

"Betsy's indomitable spirit will make you regret you ever whined about anything. And, her strength, fortitude, and faith will inspire you to march through an army of misfortunes. I laughed, cried, and was deeply moved by both Betsy and her book. Read it! Buy copies for everyone you know."

-*Todd Uterstaedt*
Founder, "From Founder To CEO"

"Betsy Craig is an amazing woman. This book is an inspiration to those impacted by scleroderma as well as entrepreneurs and business women everywhere. She is a true testament that anything can be overcome and that we can all achieve our goals in life with passion, integrity, facing our fears and persistence. Betsy has served as a board member of the Scleroderma Foundation Rocky Mountain Chapter and participates in the chapter's annual "Stepping Out to Cure Scleroderma" Walks to support the mission of the Scleroderma Foundation."

-*Cyndy Besselievre*
Executive Director Scleroderma Foundation
Rocky Mountain Chapter

"Having worked with Betsy for nearly six years, I can speak first-hand how her business practices and overall mindset have led our company to be unstoppable. This book is a must-read for anyone wanting to take their business to the next level."

-*Claire Willis*
Director of Nutrition, MenuTrinfo®

"A remarkable story of resilience, determination, and courage. Betsy Craig takes you on her journey from living as a barely functioning, self-destructive alcoholic, to a fatal diagnosis giving her 18 months to live, to being the CEO of a million-dollar company. This inspiring book gives you principles to live by, great stories that illuminate her points, and provocative questions to help you apply these principles to your own life. A must read."

-*Ava Diamond*
CEO of Ava Diamond International, Speaker on Leadership and High Performance

Michele ~ Stay Unstoppable my friend!

Unstoppable

A RECIPE FOR SUCCESS IN LIFE AND
BUSINESS

Betsy Craig

Betsy

BCGA, Press
Fort Collins, Colorado

BCGA Press
155 North College Ave Suite 208
Fort Collins, CO 80524

Ordering Information:
Quantity sales. Special discounts are available on quantity purchases by corporations, associations, and others. For details, contact the "Special Sales Department" at the address above.

Unstoppable: Betsy Craig. —1st ed.
ISBN: 978-0-6920952-4-9

I tried to recreate events, locales and conversations from my memories of them. In order to maintain their anonymity in some instances, I have changed the names of individuals and places. I may have changed some identifying characteristics and details, such as physical properties, occupations, and places of residence. I have made every effort to ensure the accuracy of the information within this book was correct at time of publication. I do not assume and hereby disclaim any liability to any party for any loss, damage, or disruption caused by errors or omissions, whether such errors or omissions result from accident, negligence, or any other cause.

Contents

Oh yes, I am wise
But it's wisdom born of pain
Yes, I've paid the price
But look how much I gained
If I have to, I can do anything

HELEN REDDY

Why I Wrote This Book

When my life bottomed out because of addiction and alcoholism in my late teens, bringing me to the brink of death, my strength and desperation led me to seek help and allow others to pull me out. So, when life threw me a huge curve-ball with scleroderma, an often-fatal progressive auto-immune disease, my strength and that will to live I learned from becoming sober allowed me to beat the odds with this miserable disease. When I started a new business following a recession, my strength and desire to succeed pushed me through 16-hour work days to get the company off the ground.

I never set out to be a CEO, but here I am running a million-dollar company; that's a long way from serving as Vice President of my daughter's middle school PTA. It blows my mind to think about where I am today, and I want others to see that if I can do it, they can do it too. I don't have an MBA, Master's Degree in food safety, or even an undergrad degree from a 4-year institution, but I do have a set of principles I live by, a deep passion to help others, a drive to learn, and a core belief that I must make a difference with this one precious life I have been given.

Through my story and experiences, I want to inspire others with an idea or passion to know that they too can do and become anything they want, to build a business, to overcome challenges, and to never give up. I have experienced first-hand the amazing opportunities that appear when staying open to all the possibilities. My intention is to provide hope, strength, and other tools to help on your journey. I am not here to tell anyone what to do because we all travel our own unique paths to success. But I do hope by sharing my story, while holding nothing back, it will inspire you to be strong in your challenges and pursue your own unique dreams in your one precious life as well.

Through passion and a set of ten spiritual principles I learned during my young adult years, I am changing the food service industry and making my positive mark on it, hopefully for many years to come. These principles taught me anything is possible. Whether it was letting go of alcohol and drugs, fighting a disease that wanted me dead, or starting a new business, these principles worked in all these areas. They have shaped me into who I am today and gave me the ingredients I needed for success.

Spiritual Principles

Passion
Integrity
Self-Support
Ask for Help
Persistence
Courage
Wisdom
Honesty
Unity

Gratitude

In each chapter, I will unpack and explore one of these principles. As you read, you may find it helpful to have a journal or notepad nearby. As your own thoughts, ideas, and insights arise, jot those down. At the end of each chapter is section called, *Food for Thought.* This is place for you to stop and reflect on the stories, ideas, and principles I shared and to think about how they relate to your life.

It is my desire that you begin integrating some or all of these principles into your business and into your life. I am living proof that by doing so, your world will open up to new possibilities you may have never dreamed of before. New opportunities, new mentors, and new ideas will flow into your life at the precise time you need them. You get back what you put out there. By allowing these principles to guide you, your life can be full and more abundant, setting you on a path to become unstoppable.

Honoring that great radio personality, Paul Harvey, and taking his well coined phrase ... here is "the rest of the story."

CHAPTER 1

Not Dying

Looking back today, I know Scleroderma prepared me to believe I can do anything or at least give it my all in trying. Doctors gave me a death sentence, but I refused to listen. I fought back because that's what I do. When life pushes against me, I push back harder. Which is why, on the heels of the global financial crisis of 2010, I started a business in a field largely uncharted. Many thought I was crazy, but when you have walked through hell like I have, it is all a matter of perspective.

I've experienced excruciating pain, had medical treatments that would take down the strongest of people, and faced, head on, a disease that wanted me dead. It is a miracle I am still here, and because of that, I realize there isn't anything in my business I can't handle. Nothing comes close to what I have been through with Scleroderma. It is this perspective that makes me a good CEO and is the key reason my company is so successful today.

Death Sentence

The first 39 years of my life, I was the picture of health. Active, in good shape, and never needed more than an aspirin for a headache. Then all of that changed. A disease I didn't know about silently attacked my body. After only a couple of months, my symptoms went from mild to severe. The worst part was my hands. It felt like somebody stuck a straw under my skin, blew air in there, and made them swollen and hard as rocks. My hands ballooned, swelled, and became so tight the skin wouldn't move at all. Then my fingertips started to rot from the outside in. My pointer fingers and my middle fingers had skin ulcers called infractions. Parts of the skin would fall off and then the skin underneath would turn dark, greenish-black from the gangrene. The physical pain was excruciating, unlike anything I had ever experienced before. Mentally, I had no idea how to go on.

I would wake up in the middle the night screaming in pain, crying and begging my husband to have the doctors cut my fingers off. The two Fentanyl Transdermal (Morphine) patches I wore all the time, along with a laundry list of other types of drugs, were meant to help me maintain some kind of quality of life with less pain. They weren't working.

In 2005, my life changed. I remember watching the nurse practitioner read a document in my file, look down at the ground, then shake her head as she matter-of-factly told me, "It's not good. You have Scleroderma, and given the type, you have 12-18 months to live. I recommend you get your affairs in order."

She confirmed what I had guessed, I had Scleroderma. A disease I could hardly pronounce let alone understand. She explained there were things they could *try,* but it didn't look promising. I couldn't believe what I was hearing. I wanted to yell at her—to shake her. *Try?* This was my life, not some new flavor of ice-cream. Her tone and her actions gave me no hope that anything they would *try* was going to work. I remember thinking that great advice from Yoda, "Try? There is NO try." A saying from one of my awesome mentors also ran through my head, *Honey, try means lie. Just do it.*

This was the moment I learned all the pain and suffering I had endured the past of couple years was a result of scleroderma, a rare disease which caused the hardening and tightening of the skin and connective tissues. "Sclero" means hard, and "derma" means skin. My type (diffuse systemic scleroderma) was tough to treat because it had already started to attack my body, not only on the outside, but on the inside as well. My lungs, GI track, and eventually my heart would be adversely affected. There is NO KNOWN cure. The prognosis was grim.

I left there terrified and convinced I would be dead in 12 months. Once I got in my car, I sat there crying. I didn't want to die. One year was not very long. What could I do in those 12 months? I wanted to see my daughter graduate from high school; I wanted to grow old with Rocky, my husband of two years. I was only 41 years old, and I was not done, not by a long shot.

After two long years of not knowing, I finally had a diagnosis and was told I had, at most, 18 months to live. Trying to wrap my brain around what the outcome might be proved more than my head and heart could handle at that moment. When I got home from the appointment, I rushed into Rocky's arms. He comforted and consoled me while I explained what the nurse practitioner had said. Rocky is an engineer and always good at analyzing a problem to find a solution. The deeper the problem, the more of a challenge he saw, and the more determined he became to find a solution.

Although he couldn't make the disease go away, he did help me calm down and said, "We will figure this out together. One step at a time, one doctor at a time."

That evening I needed my life to feel as normal as possible. Usually I met with my like-minded friends on that night of the week, so I hopped in my car and off I went. Rocky was incredible at addressing my immediate concerns, but now I needed someone to help me with my long-term fears. On the way to the meeting, I pulled over on the side of the road and called my daughter's father, my former husband, who lived 1,800 miles away in Maryland. Even though we were divorced, we always kept a strong and ongoing mutual respect for each other. We had an agreement that even if the marriage didn't work, we would remain friends. Choosing to be co-parents to our much-loved daughter as a top priority.

I explained to Dennis, my daughters' dad, that I was seriously sick with a fatal, progressive disease I had never heard of, and I had 12-18 months. He knew I had been extremely sick the previous few years and was, of course, concerned.

"You need to take our Vicky and raise her," I told him.

"Betsy," he said. "You may in fact have a fatal, progressive disease that wants you dead, but I know you, and I'm not buying it. You keep her there with you."

"But I can't do it. Didn't you hear me? I am going to die."

"I heard you. But you are going to raise her, watch her graduate high school, and then so much more. You are a good mom, and it will be okay."

My Early Years

In a strange way, I think my childhood prepared me to fight this disease, and the disease taught me to believe I must reframe my vision of myself, my abilities, and my mission. My childhood made me a fighter, one who doesn't give up, and showed me how to live life being unstoppable.

I was a kid who grew up on the right side of the tracks with parents who, in the long run, made me tougher and stronger.

My childhood can be best described as being dragged up instead of raised. To the outside world, our family seemed normal, but from the inside, it was insanity pretty much every single day. I grew up in upstate New York. My parents both had PhD's and were incredibly book smart folks. Early on, Mom was a school teacher, then she went to law school at 39 years old and became a lawyer and judge. Dad was a mathematician who taught statistics at Syracuse University before becoming an industrial psychologist. But outside of work, they both suffered. My father was a raging alcoholic, and my mother had deep and serious mental illness along with rheumatoid arthritis.

We had the money we needed as a family to keep up the outside image. However, all the money in the world couldn't stop what happened behind closed doors—alcoholism, all types of abuse, the things my parents said to me, and even more challenges due to my undiagnosed learning disorder. At an early age, I had to learn to stand on my own two feet and not rely on help or support from the adults in my life who should have been there for me.

I have a saying I learned in my 20's that helps me avoid becoming a victim to my history: *look back, but don't stare*. That's how I feel about my childhood—the parts I remember, anyway (there is a lot I have blocked out, thank God!). As a result, it has made me a stronger person today.

Rippin' and Runnin'

My drinking and drugging started when I was 13. But when I hit 16, my foot slammed down on the throttle of life, and I drove full bore toward self-destruction, indulging in bad choices every day. No one could tell me what to do. I ran around until all hours of the night and morning, staying out for a week at a time, proving nobody could make me go home. It was more peaceful if I wasn't there anyway, and the insanity going on between my folks meant they didn't care.

After living 11 years in the same house, and my entire life in central New York, my parents moved us hours away to Columbia, Maryland, for my senior year of high school. Dad had lost his job teaching at SU and found a new career in Washington, DC. Even though circumstances allowed him to wait one more year for me to finish 12th grade in the place where I had spent my entire academic career, I was uprooted. Everything familiar, everything I knew, went away. My answer was to completely zone out and rip and run even more by drinking and drugging harder, being more disruptive at home and at school, and increasing my already intense rebellion up a notch. I became unstoppable in a very unhealthy and self-destructive way.

In June of 1982, at 17 years old, I graduated, and within a week, I moved out of my parent's home. Quickly, I found my happy place working in the bar business, as these were and continue to be my kind of people. I simply love food service folks! Toughness and strength are prerequisites for success in the hospitality industry. It's a work hard, play hard type of mentality. I was tough. I am still tough, but I was tough and stupid back then. I worked 60+ hours a week and found myself surrounded by big-money, crazy drinkers, drugs, music, power, and prestige. It was an absolute breeding ground for insanity, and it fit me like a glove. I had found my home.

My day started at 4:00 in the afternoon where I was a waitress, tended bar, and even worked as a DJ. We'd close-up around 2:00 am and then have our own party. At six or seven in the morning, I'd stagger home, pass out for a few hours only to wake up and do it all again. I lived in a constant stream of humiliation, denial, and regret, having to apologize for the words and actions I could remember taking place while I was wasted. All the drugs and alcohol caused big chunks of time to be lost without any recollection of what happened. Since this was a time before text messages, twitter, or social media, there was no record for me piece the lost bits of time together. I was slowly killing myself, one day at a time. For three plus years, this destructive schedule ruled my life. I felt powerless to care and do anything about alcoholism and addiction.

About half way through my 20th year of life, a moment of clarity hit me. I think God spoke to my heart, *If you keep going like this, there is not going to be much left of you.* I barely functioned. My life had been spinning completely out of control, and something needed to change.

In 1984, I watched my dad stop drinking with the help of some newfound friends and saw how much it changed his personality for the better. It inspired me and gave me hope that maybe, just maybe, I could do the same thing.

On May 3rd of 1985, it became clear to me that I stood at a jumping off point in my life, and the time was right. So, I took a leap of faith and did something that still serves me well today in life and business. I asked for help. When I summoned the courage to finally reach out, I went to where folks go to get help to stop drinking and drugging. The heroes there welcomed me with open arms and accepted me exactly where I was.

They gave me a cup of coffee and said, "Sit down, honey."

"We understand how you feel."

"Time to suit up, show up, and grow up."

"Let us take you for ice cream; everything is always better with ice cream."

"We're going to give you new tools and teach you how to be a sober person."

With their help, I found a daytime sales job in the restaurant industry I already knew so much about. Unlike the bar scene, it allowed me to pursue healthier life habits. I began creating a new normal for myself and got by with a little help from my new group of friends. Using the new tools they introduced me to, along with spiritual help, my thoughts shifted from drinking and drugging to pulling myself together to become a different Betsy. Even though it hasn't been a piece of cake, from that day forward, I have been sober every day since and no longer rely on alcohol or other drugs to help me cope with my problems.

As I got older, life settled down. I had my daughter, got married, and I was determined to be the mother I never had. I wanted my daughter to know she was safe, loved, and the most important person in the world to me. But even though I went through the actions and said all the right things, deep down in my core, rage simmered, and a sense the world owed me still lurked in my thoughts.

Finding Hope

As I hung up the phone with Dennis, I sat in the car and lost it. Sobs wracked my body as I processed all of it. But despite the devastation of this news, the words from both Rocky and Dennis looped in my mind, and I started to think maybe they were right. After all, these two men knew me better than anyone else in this world and knew I was tough. Maybe, just maybe, I could fight this disease and beat this terminal diagnosis.

Sitting there in the car, I experienced every emotion possible. I wondered how this happened. Did I do something to bring this on myself? For the next three months, I allowed myself to wallow in self-pity and be so mad at God I couldn't see straight. I wanted to know why He brought me here, just to drop me on my ass. I kept thinking, *Are you kidding? This is it? Screw you!* (I have a God big enough that I can say "screw you," and God's cool with it, and I'm cool with it).

Being an advocate for my own health care, treatment, and game plan became the number one priority in my life. It was time to take the principles that got me sober and apply them to living with the disease of scleroderma and focus on one day at a time. Using the idea of getting help from others, I joined the support group for those living with Scleroderma. I went to listen, learn, and eventually give back. I went doctor shopping, in the best possible sense of this term, until I found the one who refused to throw in the towel.

He looked at me and said, "Yes, it's systemic sclerosis scleroderma. But I won't give up."

Right then, I knew I found my next doctor. I finally met somebody who believed I could live, making all the difference in the world. He didn't want to cut my fingers off, and by then, they were black. He was willing to try a radical procedure to open up every blood vessel in my body with the hopes of restoring circulation down to the tips of my fingers. To my relief and joy, it worked.

Although the gangrene had healed, the scleroderma was now killing me from the inside out. My hands felt like immobile claws. I couldn't button or zip up my own pants, could not do normal self-care like brush my hair or shave my legs. I couldn't even take the lid off a to-go cup of coffee. My face was so tight that my ears were pulling away at the earlobe, and blood would drip down the sides of my face daily. My skin felt as hard as stone and was hypersensitive to touch. If someone barely bumped me, I'd start crying because the pain was intensified from the nerves now resting on the edge of my skin. I walked around feeling like a leper. Not being able to hug my daughter or husband without it causing excruciating pain devastated me. I desperately wanted to give up but knew if I did that, I'd be dead.

To say my marriage, now only three-years old, was not going as planned was an understatement. Neither Rocky nor I signed up for this. In sickness and in health is easy to say when all appear healthy, but I married the perfect partner for me. He believed I would recover and be OK no matter what the medical community told me. His love, strength, and determination helped me whenever we received news from the doctor that scared me. At times though, I could see it made him angry because he couldn't fix it or sad because he didn't want to lose me. Who could blame him? I was wasting away before his eyes, but he was intent on finding answers and new options at every turn.

I went to the University of Colorado Hospital Scleroderma clinic and met my new doctor. It is an amazing teaching hospital in Denver, Colorado.

"I need a new course of action," I told the doctor. "I have to watch my daughter graduate from high school in 2009. I will do anything to stay alive three more years to see that happen."

He said, and I will never forget the exact words as long as I get to live, "How would you feel if we hit you with the bus?"

"You can hit me with the biggest bus you have, if it will keep me alive. I am willing to do anything if it gives me a chance. I am all in."

He wasn't kidding about the impact and harshness of this new treatment. It sent me back to my couch where all I could do was concentrate on not dying. Every day I woke up, I would try to focus on one small thing I would try to do each day. It gave me an entirely new appreciation for one of my favorite slogans, *One Day at a Time*.

Months went by. I had fought scleroderma for two years and finally started feeling a little better. I knew I had a choice to make, as I stood at another turning point: *get up and do something with my life or die there on the couch*. Considering all the pain I had dealt with, nobody would blame me if I gave up. The doctors already said I would die, so if I stayed right on that couch, they would be right.

One day, I laid there on my comfortable blue sectional, the chemo coursing through my body, and something inside me shifted. I felt the shift deep to my core, but could not describe it then or now, other than to say, I believe it was God. The sun streamed through the big windows, filling the room with warm light. Then God whispered in my ear. *I got you. You're not going to die.*

In the past, I used to make deals with God: if you get me out of this one, I will stop drinking; or if you get me home safely, I won't be so out of control. I didn't keep those deals, but this one was different. On this day, I made a fresh deal with God. I said, "If you get me off this couch, I am not going to stop. I will do something worthwhile with this one precious life, if you will let me keep it."

A warm, loving energy surged through me, and I knew I would never be the same. I was filled with something I hadn't felt in a long time—hope.

In that moment, everything changed.

All of the angry, east coast, self-indulgent person inside of me disappeared. I lost the entitled attitude weighing on my shoulders from a childhood of abuse and neglect. I knew I was not going to die like the nurse practitioner said I would, and I decided to start living again, beginning that moment.

Moving Forward

Physically, I still couldn't get off the couch super easily, and it still hurt like hell. But on that day, I left it mentally.

I had been telling my daughter for years the importance of a college degree, and I felt like a hypocrite knowing I didn't have one. Even though I could only type with a couple fingers because the rest still would not move, physically driving to campus and attending classes was hard, and each key stroke contained pain and discomfort, I took a few courses each semester. Some in person and some online. It was possible if I remained willing to be gentle with myself but not quit no matter what. I had chemo brain, dyslexia, and my hands and body worked against me physically, but I just kept telling myself one step, key stroke, or class at a time. Working toward the degree gave me purpose and something to strive toward. I knew if I could move on with my life, I would be unstoppable.

In 2007, I received my general business degree and entered back into the work force, ready to make a difference in this world. For the first time in my life, I worked for a small startup company in the technology space. In 2009, I beamed with pride as I watched my baby girl graduate from high school. She got the short end of the stick, thanks to my illness, but I sure did my best.

My crazy smart daughter entered college with my full support and quickly those expenses came due. Thank goodness I had been well enough to work to support her school dreams. Everything went along great until, out of nowhere, I was fired and found myself unemployed. Sure, I was blessed to be married to my wonderful soulmate of a husband, Rocky, who was gainfully employed and had income stability, supporting me during those years I couldn't work, but I still had my obligations.

Fortunately, I secured another job and began right away. Less than one month there, I discovered two of the three partners in the new business used medical marijuana, which is legal in my state of Colorado. As someone who chose to give up alcohol and drugs, being around it on a daily basis was not something I wanted. Each day I would go home smelling like weed. This was not what I envisioned for my life. They didn't love my displeasure with their legal pot use very much either and fired me.

Around this time, I also got a message from a friend on Facebook. This ended up being the industry changing idea I would soon pursue as my new business. This friend mentioned I should start a business dealing with menu labeling and food safety because it was part of the Affordable Healthcare Act going into effect one day in the near future.

She knew my husband was a software engineer and said, "Betsy, you and Rocky should look into this and see if he can make a software to do this very thing."

After a few days of letting this idea marinate, I reached back to her. "Thanks for the idea. I do love it. Are you okay if I move forward with it to start a business?"

"Go for it! Make it a million-dollar business," she responded.

For years I had noticed that in addition to taking medications to deal with my disease, other things played into how I felt. Holistic treatments like yoga and massage helped, but the food I ate or didn't eat had a massive impact on my body. I started paying attention to ingredient lists and appreciated restaurants with the same level of attentiveness to their menus. My basic rule was if I could not pronounce the ingredient, I would not eat the food. Highly processed foods went away almost completely as did sodas and such.

What most people would see as a bad thing, being fired from my job, turned out to not be so bad at all. This change in my employment future pushed me toward my newfound mission of finding an easier way for restaurants to provide nutritional information to their customers. As co-founders, my husband and I set out to make this happen. Rocky used his software development skills and expert database knowledge to create the nation's leading nutritional software for the food service industry. He got permission from his full-time employer to run with the idea, but it had to be on his personal time. Since his job kept us going both financially and provided us with amazing health insurance, he had to stay. Using the USDA database as the core, he created software that drilled down into each component/ingredient of a recipe to identify nutrients, all levels of food allergens, and create solutions for menu labeling.

While he worked on the tech side of it, I stepped into my role of CEO and created a business model for us to use. On a cold February afternoon in 2010, around our kitchen table, MenuTrinfo® (the name is a mashup of the words menu, nutrition, and information) was born with me at the helm.

Not long after, in 2011, thanks to the delay of menu labeling and therefore the delay of the clients needing my business, I pivoted to include a ground-breaking program, AllerTrain™. Developed to train food service professionals about food allergies and Celiac Disease, AllerTrain™ provides them the knowledge to better accommodate customers with special dietary needs.

Over the years, my company has helped major restaurant chains you drive by each day to provide the best service possible to their customers who may or may not have life threatening food allergies. In addition, we have worked with hundreds of university dining halls and kitchens across the country to teach them about those same allergies and the need for Gluten-Free options. This side of the food service industry has been hit extremely hard with the need for training and assistance because they serve the same students with special dietary needs, day in and day out. These young adults are a vulnerable population due to being on their own for the first time in their young lives and having to navigate and advocate for themselves. It can be the biggest nightmare or wonderful success story depending upon the university or college. The ones using our ANSI (American National Standards Institute) accredited training program definitely have great success stories to share.

When I chose to bootstrap the business, I knew it meant some sacrifices. I would not be able to pull a salary right away, my office was our 900-square foot empty-nester basement, and I had to figure out how to make it work in a way that didn't involve cold hard cash because that was always in short supply. Thankfully, my first paying clients came in June of 2010, a short five months from the day the idea came from Facebook. Today MenuTrinfo® is a strong, majority woman-owned, cash flow positive for many years, million-dollar company with a dozen+ employees who all make a living wage with great health care.

Scleroderma is still active in my body, but I do not allow it to control my life. Although each case of scleroderma is different, if you try to compare me to other scleroderma patients, I'm a walking, breathing miracle. I should be functioning two or three hours a day, maybe. All of the folks in my original scleroderma support group have passed away except for me and one other. But instead of sitting at death's door, I have this abundance of energy, an insatiable thirst for life, and nothing is going to stop me.

Getting off the Couch

We all have our own "couches." It may not be a physical one, but it's something that holds us back. My mom's rheumatoid arthritis and mental illness kept her trapped on our living room couch in my childhood and then later in life for her for long periods of time. My dad's alcoholism landed him on the couch, drunk and passed out, way more times than I could count. In fact, when he was there, I knew at least there would be peace until he awoke.

In my 20s, I rose from my own alcoholic and drug addicted couch. When scleroderma hit me and knocked me down, I was determined to not let my disease confine me there forever. I did not want to be one who gave up on myself or on my future. Many of the principles and lessons I learned in my life, in partnership with a strong spiritual faith, are what gave me the strength to move. To get up.

With this strong, conscious, and unstoppable decision, my life changed forever. Suddenly, I felt like a different person. The anger that consumed me in my youth, and rested just below the surface in my 20s, disappeared. It was as if a light switch was flipped, and today I find it incredibly hard to explain except to say I no longer felt the world owed me. Self-seeking went away on a whole different level. I shifted my thinking from *How can you help me?* to *How can I help you?* But more on that later.

We all have the power to get off our own couch, move past the doubts and the fear toward a more fulfilling life. All it takes is that first step. The spiritual principles in this book can help you take that step and all the steps that follow.

Food for Thought

➢ Reflect on your life. Think about three challenging life events and what you learned from each of those.

➢ How did those events impact who you are today?

➢ What does that small voice of doubt say to you that keeps you stuck in a job, in a marriage, in a position or role in your life?

➢ What is the truth about what you wish you could do with your one precious life?

➢ As I mentioned at the end of the chapter, we all have a "couch." Something that holds us back from reaching our full potential. What is your couch? Take a moment to write down how your life would be different if that couch was no longer there

CHAPTER 2

Passion Alone Won't Pay the Rent

Spiritual Principle: Passion

pas·sion (noun) a strong liking or desire for or devotion to some activity, object, or concept

Passion. It inspires people to practice an instrument for hours on end. It's the underlying motivation behind an Olympic athlete training to be the best. It can also be the fuel between incredibly damaging crimes and ill will. Most, if not all of us, have probably seen passion do amazing things and horrific things. It is two different sides of the same coin. For me, it's the driving force behind my company. It's what propelled me to work 16+ hour days, seven days a week, in the beginning and still some days today. It got my business launched, going, and what keeps it strong today. But passion, without being followed by purpose, will simply burn out.

I found my personal life's passion from *not* dying from scleroderma, from getting up off that couch and stepping into a new calling, but with a mission and drive like I had never experienced before. I had been given this incredible gift of life, and

I wanted to use it to be of service in a new and different way to countless others, strangers and friends I had not met yet.

You Are What You Eat

My company is a nutritional help desk looking at what restaurants are serving America on a plate or in a paper sack. Because such a huge part of my business assists those with food allergies, people always ask me if I have a food allergy. I don't. But my choices on what I put into my body have changed for the better. I cannot remember the last time I had a cola, and I used to drink many of them daily. When I was trying to recover from the initial impact of Scleroderma, 95% of the time, I lived by the rule that if I couldn't pronounce an ingredient on the nutritional fact panel of a food item or beverage, it would not pass by my lips. This was one of the major ways my diet and food choices changed. I had to learn some basic fundamentals of nutrition.

On days when I felt great, I paid attention to what I ate that day or days before, and conversely, when it was hard to move and function, I thought about what I had eaten. Scleroderma magnified my physical condition, both good and bad, based on my food intake. My disease has nothing to do with allergies, but as with most challenges with our body, what I put into it can have a huge impact on how I feel. Food is, in fact, true health care, and medicine is sick care. I live that each and every day and pay a huge price when I have my "cheat" foods. This is a big reason I am passionate about my business and what we do.

Scleroderma is an autoimmune disease that causes someone's immune system to attack itself by creating too much collagen. This is what causes the skin and, for some with the type of scleroderma I have, internal organs to harden. Currently there is no cure, only treatments to manage symptoms. One drug that helped me turn my life around was the chemotherapy drug, Methatrexate. For 2½ years, this medication coursed through my body, suppressing my immune system in order to decrease the symptoms of the disease. Simple really, slow down the immune system, and the auto immune disease gets slowed down as well. It worked. I got the use of my hands back, but I passionately believe that the drug was only part of the reason I got better.

To give myself the best fighting chance possible, I knew it was time I made some concrete changes in my life as well. Up until I got sick at 39, I still smoked two packs of Marlboro reds a day. Since giving up alcohol and drugs at 20 years old, smoking felt like the one comfort I had left, even though I knew it wasn't good for me. When I learned that it narrows blood vessels and was not helping my situation, I was even more convinced it was time. Although it wasn't easy and took a number of attempts, I finally gave it up. One of my doctors put it in terms I could understand, he said, "I can't care more about your health then you do. Keep smoking, and I simply cannot treat you." That made me look at things a bit differently for sure.

Not personally having a food allergy allows me to be the perfect messenger. I don't get pooh-poohed as an overprotective allergy mom or someone who is just a fussy eater. Sadly, it's way too easy to dismiss a parent or somebody with food allergies as just looking out for themselves and minimizing the special dietary request.

As the CEO of MenuTrinfo®, I come at it from a business standpoint knowing the industry I grew up in from 15-years-old on. I explain to C-level folks, owners, chefs, and managers that by taking care of their customers, they are taking care of their businesses and creating a positive experience for those patrons, which in the long run, helps their companies and their bottom line.

Who Needs an MBA Anyway?

After my friend had sent me that gift of a Facebook message about menu labeling, I began to research it. I learned what companies were out there in the food industry helping restaurateurs figure out the nutrition information in the food they served and sold. I started to see bigger possibilities when Rocky pointed out that he could tag food allergens within our software, and people might want to acquire this information. He took what I was passionate about and implemented what would become the next important ingredient in my recipe for success.

The country has seen an unprecedented increase in food allergies like never before. For some, it is even a matter of life and death. That resonated with me deep to my core. Even though I don't have food allergies, I empathized with what they were going through, and I knew I could help. I wanted to stand up for those with food allergies and special diets. If I was going to be passionate about any message, it had to be a good one, and this one felt right.

Whether it's in life or business, passion alone is not enough to make a difference. My heart believes it needs to be tied to a purpose and mission. For me that became protecting lives and health, first mine, then hundreds, now thousands of others. This was something I could get behind.

A key in using passion to create a business is working towards how to monetize the mission. Now that I found myself without a job, I wanted to find a way to combine my need to pay my bills with this newfound passion surrounding food safety, followed by taking the necessary steps to make that happen.

During this interim, I collected unemployment. Having been fired and out looking for a job at the time made me eligible to collect it as long as I continued job seeking and was available for work. I was. Looking for another full-time position was a top priority, but the job never came. The unemployment checks gave me the money I needed to make ends meet, while allowing me time to research what I wanted my business to look like and how I could be of service to restaurants and consumers through menu labeling. Being 100% honest with the state and following the rules laid out to be eligible to collect the government assistance was extremely important to me as well. My passion for this new business took me down a path that I believe was divinely guided and led to the creation of Menu-Trinfo® in early 2010.

Turns out, Rocky's amazing software, my new general studies degree from the local community college, my gift for sales, and my passion created the perfect combination. What I didn't have was the knowledge and experience to run a business; the basic information to drive the passion towards success. Because, by nature, I am an unstoppable person, this didn't deter me.

I called Colorado State University.

"My name is Betsy Craig, and I am interested in going through your MBA program."

"Great," said the woman on the other end of the phone. "Let me get a little bit of information from you. Where did you get your bachelor's degree?"

"I don't have one." I paused and waited for her to speak. She didn't, so I said, "I desperately need the information taught in the business classes. Can I just sit in on them?" I asked.

"Um, no ma'am," she said. "You actually need a four-year degree before you can begin an MBA program."

"Darn it! That really stinks."

"Yes, it does," she said. "But that's how it works. We can't let you in."

I smiled, "But you should let me in."

"I know, but we can't," she said. I could sense her holding back her laughter.

"I understand," I said. "Thanks for your time. I guess I'll have to figure something else out."

I hung up. My brain reeled as it tried to come up with a new plan. I knew I needed help and the tools necessary to run a successful business. When I quit drinking, my mentors taught me that if I was willing to do the hard work, I could do anything. Believing in this mission of food safety with my entire being, I knew I could take this passion and somehow, someway, make it happen. It was time to pray and trust that an answer would appear.

The next day, I came across a brochure for the Rocky Mountain Innosphere (RMI), a local business incubator, that was offering something called FastTrac® by Kauffman. From their website, it was described as a program that "equips aspiring entrepreneurs with the business skills and insights, tools, resources, and peer networks necessary to start and grow successful businesses." This was exactly what I needed. This five-week program began in a few weeks and included two classes per week.

FastTrac® included basic skills and tools a CEO of a brand-new start-up would need to know. The information was laid out in a fast, simple, and clear way. It was real people telling their stories on a variety of topics I desperately needed. Topics included:

- Exploring Your New Business
- Identifying and Meeting Market Needs
- Setting Financial Goals
- Planning Your Product/Service
- Reaching and Analyzing the Market
- Reaching the Market
- Building Your Organization and Team
- Planning for a Profitable Business
- Cash Flow and Acquiring Funds
- Implementing Your Plan

It was like a mini-MBA. I wasted no time in applying. A few weeks later, while sitting in a hotel room in Beijing, China watching Obama sign in the Affordable Care Act (which contained menu labeling legislation), I got an email from RMI, "Congratulations! You have been accepted into the FastTrac® program. Send RMI (which is now called the Fort Collins Innosphere) the $999 class fee, and you can join us at the first class next Wednesday."

I went from elated to deflated in a matter of seconds. I was thrilled that I had been accepted but then disappointed because of the cost. With my new business having launched only a month before and no extra income coming in, I didn't have the $999 needed to sign up for the program and really could not justify taking that kind of cash from our household, considering my lack of income.

I emailed them back, "I am super excited about this opportunity; but unfortunately, I don't have the money for it at this time. I really wish I could do it because it sounds like exactly what I need right now. Have a good class, and if you offer it again in the future and I have the money, I will reapply."

Less than an hour later, I got an email back from them, "We have obtained a scholarship from the Larimer County Workforce Center. Since you are unemployed, they are willing to pay for the class. Can you still join us next Wednesday?"

My heart jumped; I jumped.

"Woo-hoo!" I sent back my reply. "Yes, I will be there. Thank you!"

The program turned out to be exactly what I needed. They broke us up in to smaller groups for more one on one class study based on our industry. There were four people in mine and two business coaches. We were the "misfits" because our businesses didn't fit into any specific area like alternate energy. In my great small group, there was a woman who had business software she was trying to decide if she wanted to take out into the market, one guy who was all about electric motorcycles, a young man deeply into robotics, and me with my menu labeling.

We had a wonderful group full of passionate entrepreneurs, each with our own drive. I learned so much about creating an effective company. Not only did I learn the nuts and bolts of running a business, it connected me with some amazing people who I am still in contact with today. The two coaches continued to be there for me for a number of years, providing amazing business advice, and in one case, friendship further down the road. The young man who was into robotics ended up co-founding a company in Boulder, Colorado. He and his business partner went on to do great things in robotics in the movie, toy, and tech industry. He is a great guy, and we have stayed friends despite us both having crazy busy lives. His company is incredibly successful and on this amazing trajectory, making millions and millions. My business has had more of a steady climb and finally broke that million-dollar bench mark in 2017. We have very different models of companies, but we are still able to help and lean on each other.

Learning business principles and meeting amazing people through this program would not have been possible if I had given up after CSU told me no. My passion and mission for my new company combined with my unstoppable drive, allowed me to keep moving and push through this minor setback.

Don't allow challenges along the way to stop you. They may be small bumps or big hills, but regardless, you have to keep going. Use that fuel from your passion to drive you to the top. Speed doesn't matter. What matters is that you persevere and continue moving forward.

It's Not About Me

I use the power of my passion combined with the mission and purpose of my business to be the voice for that little girl who died after simply eating a cookie on the school playground. Or the young college freshman who accidentally ingested an allergen and drove himself to the hospital, thinking he could make it, and ended up passing away in his car in the parking lot of that ER, never making it inside for help. Or the college student with celiac disease who needs to know the specific ingredients in the food served at the dining hall on campus, so she doesn't get sick and stuck in bathroom during finals week. Or the boy in a Virginia restaurant who was kicked out on a school trip because he brought his own safe food to eat for lunch, and the place simply did not know how to accommodate him while staying within the rules and laws of the food code. It breaks my heart.

What that boy needed was compassion, not condemnation. Those in the food-service and hospitality industries must be informed and trained so they can better understand and meet the needs of those with special diets, showing them kindness and respect. This is why I will go anywhere to work with and train anyone willing to, as my husband coined the phrase, "keep the hospital out of hospitality."

The nutrition side is where we are affecting change for millions of people each and every day. By detailing the nutritional information, customers on special diets or those conscientious about their food can stay informed. I know how much it helped me when I started being more aware of the food I ate.

By providing not just the calories, but the carbohydrates, it matters to diabetics; by sharing the sodium numbers, it matters to heart patients. It's all part of the bigger picture. It doesn't matter if it is a sub sandwich at a national chain or popcorn at the local movie theater, when people go out and enjoy a night with their family, they seek information for their physical health and safety. We provide the nutritional data to our clients, who then provide to the public in tens of thousands upon of locations across the country. They can't get that accurate information without companies like ours, and there aren't many.

Spreading the Message

Regularly, I get asked to speak at conferences and trade shows around the country. There are a lot of people passionate about food safety, but to be an articulate conveyor of the message from the front of the room takes a different personality. It might be from my early years of being a DJ, the decades I've been in sales, or because I have the gift of the gab, but whatever the reason, I've been told numerous times I take complicated information, laws, and pending legislation and make it simple for people to understand (and I make them laugh) all while explaining why it's good for their business. They hear the passion I have about keeping people safe, and the message comes through loud and clear.

That's why I get asked back to speak year after year and how we get a lot of our new clients. These opportunities allow me to continue to share my personal story as well as my passion, and they have a positive impact on the industry.

Passion Got the Job Done

A large railroad company in our country was seeking a solution to provide accurate and complete nutritional information, allergen charts, and training for their 26 menus on all the different train services throughout the country. They put out a RFP (request for proposals) to find the right provider, and we submitted one. I was thrilled when were picked as one of four companies to go visit them at their home office in the Mid Atlantic part of the country to present our case as to why we were the best company to do the job.

My Director of Nutrition for MenuTrinfo®, Claire, came with me for a number of reasons. She knows our software like the back of her hand, can explain the process much better then I, and she could also assist in keeping me grounded and on point when needed. Sometimes my passion gets me so excited that it is hard for me to contain myself. Given how big a deal I knew this could be, I wanted to present the most complete picture for the panel and in the best way possible.

We flew into Baltimore and took a train north to the potential client. Even though it would have taken less time, I decided you don't drive or take a plane to a meeting with a train transportation company. At the meeting, I shared my story of surviving scleroderma, how making better food choices helped me, and why I was so passionate about nutrition and allergies.

A few days later I received a call. The gentleman said, "Thanks for the great presentation. I am calling to let you know you got the bid."

"That is awesome," I said. "Was it because we were the cheapest?"

"No," he said, "You weren't the cheapest, but you were by far the most passionate. We want to work with a company that cares as much about people and nutrition and allergens as you do. No one showed up with that amount of passion. No one showed up with that amount of care, and no one was willing to tell us some of the issues you found on our website that you want us to correct. You took a chance and told us the truth. We respect that."

"Thanks. We are excited to work with you as well."

The passion won the three-year contract, but it was my staff's dedication, follow through, and action that prompted a renewal of that contract for another year and now another year on top of that. They have been a constant, steady client, and it's for all the right reasons. Our prices were competitive, but the passion sealed the deal.

Giving Back

At a trade show in Dallas for the Texas Restaurant Association, I presented an AllerTrain™ class. One of the people who came was a dietician for over 150 school districts in the Dallas Fort Worth area.

This woman tracked me down after my talk. "I loved your presentation. Would you be willing to speak with all my food service directors at the start of the school year?"

"Sure. I'd be happy to," I replied.

Then she dropped the bomb. "Unfortunately, we don't have any money to pay you."

"Then I will work on getting a sponsor," I said without hesitating. "I know of a dad who has a child with allergies, and he has recently started a new foundation. I will ask him and see if he can help find the funding for this class."

A couple days later, I tracked down the gentleman, and he said he'd be glad to help by paying for my travel, the course fees, and the workbook. In the end, it was going to be about $1,500. I was thrilled that he wanted to support training the school district with this.

Then he disappeared. He stopped calling and stopped responding to my emails. Went dark as we say in the sales business. Meanwhile, I already scheduled the dates for two locations. Still bootstrapping the company, I didn't really have money to do this training. I wasn't going to let the school districts down, but most of all, I was not going to let those kids down who, in the end, would ultimately benefit.

I called the owner of a gluten-free bakery down there, Local Oven Bakery, and asked if he would be able to pay for the workbooks which were going to be about a $250 cost. He agreed.

Then I used points from my American Express I had been saving for years and bought my plane ticket. I stayed with my cousin to save on lodging expenses. The only thing it cost me out of pocket was a rental car. I went down there and trained the food service directors for two days and hand-graded every exam. I left knowing those allergy kids were now in good hands and would be taken care of.

It was passion that drove this training. Have we ever got additional business from it? Nope. We've never had any school districts in Texas come to us for additional trainings. Nor has the partnership with Local Oven gone beyond that point. But I do believe if we do the right thing for the right reason, we will reap the rewards. I have had plenty of other people and clients come to me in other ways, and I believe it is because of incidents like this.

As I said while being interviewed on a podcast, passion rocks, but it doesn't pay the rent. I have to balance it with paying clients and opportunities. I can't do Texas over and over. I have to do the railroad companies too.

Paying It Forward

Growing up, my parents were not encouraging and supportive toward me. Maybe they thought they were, but that's not how I felt. As time went on, I forgave them and moved along. Looking back, I am grateful for the lessons this taught me but less than thrilled about how I had to learn them. At an early age, I had to learn to stand on my own two feet, and although that was good in some situations, there were times I needed help from others I could count on. In my early 20s, when I decided to stop the drinking and drugging, I knew I couldn't do it on my own. When I reached out to people who had gone through the same things, they were there for me. They showed me compassion and a few of those women became my mentors. Without these strong role models, I would not be the person and business woman I am today.

As I grew and became more confident, those ladies stayed in my life, but I wanted to pay it forward. I took that passion that was poured into me and became a mentor for other women. I shared with them my experiences, strength, and hope, and I reminded them that even with the bad choices I made along the way, I learned from those. It is my desire that by sharing my story, it will help them not drink and encourage them make healthier life choices.

I continue to have a vested and personal interest in these gals who asked me to sit in the front row of their lives. The ladies have changed over time. Some stayed for years, while others stayed in my life for months or moments, but I agreed to be their coach, to have their backs, to show up and be the loudest one clapping in the audience. I want them to do well at their jobs, have a positive impact on their communities, have healthy relationships, buy homes, grow lives, and become amazingly successful, strong, confident, and loving women. It is really important to pass that along to others, to pay it forward because, spiritually, I have to give away my passion in order to keep it.

When I was so sick with scleroderma and couldn't get off my couch, along with those dearest to me, like my husband, it was all these women (my mentors and my mentees) that kept me going when I reached out for help. They showed up, did laundry, washed bathrooms, and took care of me. One made me mashed potatoes because it was the only thing I could eat for two days. They'd run errands, send cards, and encourage me over the phone. These friends showed me compassion, and it's something I hope I continue to pay forward.

So, how does this idea of being passionate for others play out from a business owner's standpoint? It allows me to model this to the dozen young women who work in my office. Everything as simple as buying everyone the book, *Lean In*, so they hear from other strong women, to studying Walt Disney's business principles and philosophies as a group, to having one-on-one meetings with my leadership team so that I can learn what's important to each individual leader. I pay attention to them and stay interested in their lives at work but also their personal lives, if they let me.

Many of these young ladies started working for me straight out of college, new to the business world. They've been watching and learning from me, and it's amazing to see them grow into strong women. When I see one of my team leaders use a principle that I have been modeling, like passion, and use it with their team members or clients, it makes me proud.

I always go back to I didn't set out to do this. When I look at the effect passion has had on my business and the effect it is has on accomplishing my mission, I am amazed. I take that energy with me when I speak and get others excited about being of service to those with food allergies and special diets. I am passionate about mentoring others, and then they pay it forward; it's a wonderful ripple.

Passion: Food for Thought

➢ Make a list of three activities, causes, or groups of people you are passionate about.

➢ List the ways you express these passions currently in your life.

➢ What are the ways you can implement these more into your life?

➢ Recall a time when you were the recipient of someone paying it forward. Now recall a time when you paid it forward. How did both of the experiences make you feel?

CHAPTER 3

Always Do What is Right

Spiritual Principle: Integrity

in·teg·ri·ty (noun) adherence to moral and ethical principles; soundness of moral character;

After living my young life on a selfish, self-centered path and NOT doing the right thing, I paid a heavy price. In my 20s, I was taught to always do the right thing to the best of my ability. Always. If someone is watching or not. Most people learn this kind of value and principle from their parents. I had to rely on others along the way. My teacher arrived in a dusty room, a lady who was just like me, a little rough around the edges, but she loved me with her whole heart. I wanted to make her proud and do what she was teaching me. Finding a way to have and show integrity became a personal goal for me.

In 1985, the year I quit drinking, my mentor and friend at the time told me, "Betsy, just remember always *you are as sick as your secrets.*"

Things that are sick don't grow, don't flourish, don't become successful. Whether that is a person, a business, or a marriage, the concept is the same. I can talk about integrity, but for that to ring true, I have to live with integrity. I choose to live my life so that if you walk behind me with a video camera, there's nothing I am doing that I wouldn't want you to see."

That's where business leaders and CEOs get jacked up constantly. They talk a really good game. Then it turns out they have a worker at home they are paying ten bucks an hour, under the table, and it comes out in the press. Or they run an amazing empire/food service company but like to hunt for exotic game, and the pictures flood the Internet, calling them out for animal cruelty. I could go on and on about companies without integrity, but I like to focus on the positive. There are more upstanding companies who exemplify the qualities of integrity. The CEOs I know, and am blessed to call friends, do walk their talk in the business community. They don't make the news as much, but they are the ones I watch and emulate because I like to stick with the winners in my industry.

Years ago, someone introduced me to an awesome gentleman who provides a top of the line e-learning platform for many different industries, hospitality being one of them. I would describe this wonderful man as a good old boy from the deep south, also one of the sweetest men I've ever met, and one of the sharpest tools in the shed. This man has the Midas touch and makes all sorts of folks better off for having met and known him.

He has a saying hanging over his door, "You will never get in trouble for helping a client." Everyone I have spoken to that knows him says he lives by these words and teaches them to others through his actions. It is one of the simplest ways I see to teach integrity to those behind me-—show it through everything I do.

As a result of his saying, I have a standard in my business that no matter what, a customer comes first or nothing else will matter. It is from leaders like him that I have learned and continue to learn how integrity strengthens a company.

For instance, we recently started offering an auditing service as part of our business. This is to ensure that commercial kitchens are food allergy safe whenever and wherever possible, if that is what they are claiming. A second set of expert eyes to review the facility is a great way for the kitchen and the consumer to be confident it is allergy safe. A company who makes allergen test kits approached us and said if we recommend their kits over others, they would either give us a kickback for each kit sold, or we could give a discount to our clients. Instantly, I said of course we want to give the discount to our clients. There is no gray area for me. Anytime I am approached about my company getting a kickback to recommend a product, the answer is no. I don't need the extra money, not if I am living with integrity. I am always thinking about what I would tell a client if every move we make as a company is transparent. Would I have any tough explaining to do?

Angel Investor

When I decided to start MenuTrinfo®, I had to figure out how to get money to start the business. I wasn't willing to jeopardize my new family and take money from our household. My option with the least amount of impact was to cash in my 401(k). The recession had hit so hard I called it my 201(k) instead. It was worth about half of what it had been just two years before. I also had to pay penalties for withdrawing the money early. It dropped the value another 40%, but at least it was something to help me start this new endeavor. So, I had this, along with stock my husband offered to sell that would not take directly from our household, a small amount in savings, and a few credit cards yet to be maxed out.

My 401(k) was a resource at my fingertips. I knew it was money I could count on that wouldn't take me further into debt. With the credit cards, I only went to those once I tapped everything else that was cash liquid. I believed the business was going to be successful, so I wasn't worried.

Operating my company with honor and integrity was important to me, especially when it came to the finances. I planned to be smart about how and where I spent my money, creating a strong foundation and base from which to build. Starting out with a large amount of debt, and overextending myself financially, was not a direction I was willing to go. In the beginning, it meant running the business from our basement. When it grew enough to move into an office, it meant sitting on folding chairs until I could afford better ones. I paid close attention and made sure I stayed realistic on the amount of money I had to spend. This lesson was taught to me by the start-up company I worked for a few years earlier. At the office, almost none of the furniture matched and the whole vibe was plain, but the company was solvent at that time. Fancy offices and big salaries to appease the egos came next, right before that business crashed. Lesson noted.

A number of people approached me about investing in my company, which would have been helpful, but none of them felt right. Taking money from just anyone would leave me handcuffed to that person. From what I had heard and learned, up until this point, about running a business, I knew I only wanted financing or investors who operated by the same basic principles I did. I stay open for answers and people to show up in my life in unexpected ways because they may have something to teach me or vice versa.

A mutual friend introduced me to a local gentleman, Greg, who was a strong, intelligent businessman, who had himself benefited from other people believing in him along the way. He had recently sold his super successful company in the restaurant industry and had done extremely well for himself.

I reached out to him and asked if we could meet. The best option for us to meet face to face was a simple American truck stop that Friday morning. During our meeting, he got my passion and understood my mission of protecting lives and health through nutrition and training. I told him he had done what I dreamed of doing, and it was why I wanted to meet him. I admired how he took on a new challenge, answered a growing need in business, connected with great clients, and lived with integrity. He appreciated my moxie and the fact that I was unstoppable in business and in life and seemed genuinely interested in my story.

"I'd like to help you out," Greg said. "I had people who worked with me early on, believed in me and my career, and now I would like to pay that back, or forward if you will. I am interested in mentoring you, if that's something you are interested in, or if you are only looking for capital, then I'd also like to talk with you about that."

I was surprised because I didn't anticipate this happening. That was not my motive at all for the meeting.

"If you need money to grow your business to the next level, and you are serious about an investor, write down how you would use the money and how much you would need. I will take a look, and we can go from there."

I smiled, "I will have something to you on Monday."

I came out of the truck stop and called Rocky on the speaker phone in the car.

"How'd it go?" he asked.

"That might be the best business meeting I've ever had," I said. "He is by far the nicest guy I have met yet. He truly understands what we are doing. He is interested in helping, and I might just accept it from him."

"What's different about him?" Rocky asked. "Why him and not the other six who have approached you?"

"I don't know why, but I trust him," I said. "He's smart, and I just trust him."

A few months prior, we had moved into our new office space because we had gotten a contract with a big theme park. I was glad to be there, but I knew I needed new phones, the website needed updating, and I wanted to hire a few key people. In order to do this, I needed more capital. I could let it grow organically, but that would take a longer time to hit some goals. Bringing on this investor would speed that up. It would be like going directly from first base to third base and bypassing second.

What sold me on him was he not only wanted to see Menu-Trinfo® succeed, but he also wanted to see me succeed. He was passionate about making the company as strong as possible by giving me the tools needed to be an effective CEO. Plus, he came from a place of honesty and integrity, which aligned with my own personal beliefs. He asked for a minority piece of the business and offered to spend time teaching me how to manage a successful company.

As a CPA and a CFO for a very large company before he started his own business, he had a wealth of experience and knowledge. I, on the other hand, had very little, especially with the financial part of it. I knew if I went off my passion alone, I might bury this business quickly by making a naive move, and I didn't want to do that. From my many years in the restaurant industry, I knew nutrition, health, and allergens were the future of menus. I had no doubt in my mind, but that alone wasn't going to make MenuTrinfo® successful. Plus, having the very best nutritional database in the world does no one any good if it only lives in our basement.

In the beginning, it wasn't easy. I was a person who could barely balance my own checkbook. In fact, for years I would call the bank a few times a week to ask about my balance and to see what checks had cleared and which ones were outstanding. I kept a running total at all times in my purse. Bouncing a check terrified me, and this was one way I knew to prevent it from happening. Hanging on to money that tightly was necessary, due to living hand to mouth for such a large part of my life during my self-destructive teen and young adult years, then later when I was a single mom struggling to cover our basic needs. Money had always been a hot button for me, and up until this point, I never truly learned how to manage it. I knew I didn't want to bring all these dysfunctional ideas and habits into the business as it grew.

For many years, Greg worked with me for a few hours each week. He taught me how to read profit and loss statements, handle tough employee situations, discuss my mission and purpose, track every penny, and not waiver for anything. He showed me how to grow the business in a healthy, stable way and think more like a CEO and less like a saleswoman. I had to shift my personal views of money, which were rooted in fear and uncertainty. Only through deep soul searching was I able to let go of that core fear and shift my thoughts to those of a successful CEO— one that said, *I know where we are financially. I know where we're going, and I know we will be fine.*

I understand numbers are the unsexy part of business. It's easy to be passionate about signing up a new client or saving a life of a child that has a peanut allergy. But without finding joy in the numbers and taking pride in ownership in those numbers, nothing else will be there. I can have the best product in the world, but if I'm not paying attention to profit and loss, odds are, we'll go under.

We have enjoyed almost four solid years of nonstop profit as a company; not gigantic profits, nobody's buying new Lamborghinis. But checks aren't bouncing, and we have no debt.

Everything is paid off each month, and I have a nice line of credit that's at zero. I know how to take care of myself more than I ever did before. Fifty percent of new businesses fail within the first five years, and I am happy to say I was not one of them.

After almost five years since we connected on this mission, Greg is still a welcome addition to the structure of the business. He does not come into the office every week anymore, although I am so thankful when he does. When issues crop up, we have a phone call, or we get together at our favorite truck stop to discuss the problem. I have met with him twice in the last month because he's been helping me work through an interesting proposition from a competitor. I am grateful for his guidance over the years and his continued willingness to share his knowledge and insight with me.

Living Wage

Employees that come on board know they will be given a salary they can count on, even during tumultuous times. I don't hire people at minimum wage. I hire people at a living wage. I can't expect my employees to be happy if their salary barely allows them to make ends meet.

I hear stories of people working full-time, but they still have to go to the food bank and can't afford health insurance. When the scleroderma made me so sick I could hardly move from the couch, I was grateful for the incredible health insurance I had through my husband's company. It paid for my treatments and medications. I don't know what I would have done if I didn't have that. Even though we are a small company, we do provide health insurance for the staff. It is the same type I have for myself through my husband's employment. What is good for me, is good for them, and vice versa. Can you imagine if I had better coverage then they did? They would know I wasn't walking my talk.

I want my employees to experience that safety net. If my company is going to be about health, it's really important to me that my people have health insurance and the ability to buy healthy food. All of that is vital, and I will do whatever it takes to make this happen.

Early on, when I had one full-time employee and a couple of part-timers, I realized there was a problem with payroll one month. The money coming into receivables wasn't going to be available in time to cover the check of my full-time employee. I was willing to do whatever it took so her paycheck wouldn't bounce. If I needed to sell plasma, I would've done that. I'm not going to break a commitment to people who are dependent on that money to pay their rent.

All my resources had been tapped out. It came down to two days before payroll, and I knew I wasn't going to make it. I had a necklace that had been given to me as a gift and I assumed was worth around $1,500. I decided I'd sell it at a pawn shop.

Having never set foot in a pawn shop before, I had no idea how it worked. I always thought of them as smarmy places that drug users and addicts went to get quick money. I didn't know what to expect, but I needed the money. That evening, I set out to get it.

At home, I rummaged through drawers and closets trying to find something to hold the necklace. I didn't want to walk in holding it in my hand. I wanted to present it well, and deep down, I guess I wanted to show that I wasn't like others who had to pawn items for money. I found a small cloth bag, dropped the necklace in, and pulled the drawstring to close it.

My heart raced, and my nerves were on overdrive as I headed to the shop. I knew pawn shops had a purpose. People need quick cash. Sometimes those people need the money for really innocent things, like making payroll.

I pulled into the parking lot. The pawn shop, which specialized in jewelry and coins, was next to a 7-Eleven. I sat in my car staring at the shop, trying to build up my courage to go in. I told myself that once I sold the necklace, I could go next door and get a Coke Slurpee, something I normally didn't have for a variety of reasons, starting with the ingredient listing. I took a deep breath and got out of my car.

The door beeped as I walked in. The store wasn't what I expected. I looked around and didn't see any shady people hanging out. It smelled clean and had a friendly, comfortable atmosphere. It looked like an ordinary shop with counters and cases that displayed jewelry and nice-looking folks milling around looking at the items for sale.

The man behind the counter said, "Can I help you?"

I felt like a failure as I pulled the necklace out and barked at him, "I need to sell this."

He looked at me and then took the necklace. I almost expected him to ask me why I was selling it and why I needed the money. But he didn't. He wasn't judging me, I was doing that to myself. He remained pleasant and professional.

"I'll give you $490 for it," he said. "I will hold it for a week, and you can come buy it back, with a few added fees, during that time. If you don't come back, it will be put out for sale."

Without hesitation I replied, "I'll take it!"

He gave me the cash, and the deal was done.

The kid-sized Coke Slurpee tasted great as I sat in my car settling myself down. With the cash in my pocket, I knew I could pay my employee. I smiled. What I originally thought of as a sad and humbling experience actually turned out to be empowering. I faced the situation head on and took care of it. I thanked God for giving me the strength to walk into the pawnshop.

The employee never knew her paycheck was in jeopardy. I could've gone to the pawn shop a week later to buy my necklace back, but I didn't see the need to do that. Even though it was a big sacrifice because that jewelry had some very fond memories attached to it, I knew it was time to let go of that relationship from the past. I was now happily married to an amazing man and making a huge impact on an industry. Hanging on to that history might in fact hold me back on some levels. It was a helpful lesson for me, and time to move on. Plus, I did get a Slurpee out of the deal.

Happy Money

A few years back, I studied with a spiritual teacher, named Alan Cohen, for a weekend retreat. The lessons learned from that experience still impact decisions I make today. In one of his books, he talks about happy money and that nobody should have anything but happy money in their life. Spiritually, it means money that's glad to be there. It's money that people pay you happily and gladly for your services rendered. When I heard this idea, I loved it and wanted to make sure to incorporate it into my business. I wanted all the money flowing through the company to be that of satisfied clients.

The nutritional portion of my business is set up with monthly payments, introduced to me by my mentor, Greg. Clients put a certain amount down and pay a certain amount each month for an agreed upon length of time, and then after that, they can stop our services if they wish.

This monthly recurring revenue is a big deal in the corporate world. It's a smart way to do business for the clients and for us. We have many clients who have chosen this option. In the past four years, we've only had two clients choose to opt off. The rest have stayed because they appreciate the services they get from us, and we are honest about everything we do. Our integrity as a company creates strong relationships, and our clients are happy to recommend us.

We did nutritionals for a company in DC. We agreed on the amount upfront and then the amount for the monthly payment. After their one-year contract finished, they didn't let us know they wanted to stop the service, so we kept charging them the monthly fee. We did this way past the initial 12 months. In fact, it went 10 more months before they noticed.

They called me and said, "You guys were supposed to stop taking the $199 a month 10 months ago. We just noticed that you've still been charging our credit card."

In the fine details of the contract, they were technically supposed to call and ask us to stop the service.

"I am so sorry," I said. "We will fix this right away. I will write you a check today, put it in the mail, and you'll have it in the next few days."

Even though I didn't feel it was 100% our fault, I took it on as ours. Regardless of who dropped the ball, I went about doing what I felt was right.

They called a week later after receiving the money. "We never expected you to do that. Thank you very much."

I think they anticipated a fight or a "let's meet halfway." I probably could've negotiated down, but I don't want anybody's money in our office and our business unless they're happy. We have never taken or kept unhappy money to this day. To me, that is corporate integrity— doing the right thing when nobody is watching or just because it is the right thing.

Rock Stars

I met a gentleman at an event five years ago who is now in the consulting business. Recently, he contacted me saying he may have a new client for me. Within two weeks, I signed this huge new client. The deal itself was worth over $20,000. As thanks for referrals, we generally share a small percentage back to the person who sends business our way, or we at least send a thank you note and a Starbucks gift card. I sent that gentleman a check with a percentage of what we made on the deal. He reached out after he received the check and said, "You have blown my mind."

He trusted me and my integrity enough to refer us to the company he had been consulting with, and now he's over the moon. He looks like a hero for recommending us. That's what I tell my employees; it is our goal to make the people who trust us look like heroes in their business world. Showing up, doing what we say we are going to do, being of service. Boom. It works.

Last week the COO and the lead operation person from a local sandwich shop that started here in Fort Collins, Colorado, came by and introduced himself.

"I am here because we now have over 20 locations," he said. "We'd like to get nutritionals done for our menu. I saw on your website that you work with a pizza brand based in Chicago."

"Yes, we do," I said. "I love that brand, and the CEO has become a dear friend of mine."

"That's great," he said. "I know the family and respect how they do business. I decided if they trust you, I should trust you."

I smiled at him. "You made the right decision. Now, my number one job is to make you look like a rock star for choosing us."

There is real integrity in business, then there is perceived integrity. There is a saying in sales that says, "Nobody gets fired by choosing IBM." The saying started less than four months after Time magazine named the computer "Machine of the Year" in its "Man of the Year" issue. It means if someone buys an IBM product or hires IBM to do a job, and it fails, it's ok because choosing IBM is still always the best option due to their reputation and integrity. I take that and say nobody gets fired for hiring my company. In fact, my goal is to make you look like a hero for bringing us onto your team. We use words like partner, friend, and team to refer to those that pay us for our services. They are much more than a sale or a customer. That is 100% of our job. If you choose to trust us, we will honor that trust completely, and you will be blown away at how good you look. We take pride in how we honor the commitment, how we honor our word, and if we say we're going to make it good, we will. That is real and not perceived integrity.

Good Karma

Today we have hundreds of master trainers across the US. Master trainers are people who have gone through our trainer program to learn proper policies and procedures for food allergy safety. They are then qualified to go out to restaurants, college campuses, or any other venues where there is food served and teach the AllerTrain™ course to the staff at those places. Master trainers are contracted workers and not employees of AllerTrain™. They invest in the training, then once they are certified to go out and instruct, either they teach at their schools/brands or work as an independent trainer. As independent trainers, they keep the majority of the fee from the courses when they teach.

We had a woman come to us and want to be a master trainer. She was a food allergy mom. This was a case when a food allergy mom had a lot of passion for her own child but did not understand the industry. My goal is to help all children, not just one. But she came to us to be a trainer, and we accepted her. This was back when participants had to fly to Fort Collins, Colorado, to become a trainer, go through two days of training, and then fly home. At that point, you were officially a master trainer of our classes.

She flew here, and right away I knew we were in trouble. During the first morning, she started to suggest edits to the class material. She didn't like some of the pictures we used and some of the content. I respect the fact that she had kept her child alive, and that's where she was coming from. But our class content went through a medical review board, and leaders in the industry such as a chef, dietary specialist, holistic doctor, dietician, and a gluten-free expert all read through it and gave their input. Then it went through the American National Standards Institute accreditation process.

We couldn't just change something because she had a unique experience with her child. I tried to explain this to her, as tactfully as possible, that morning, and again just before lunch, and again just after lunch. She went through the master trainers class, passed the test, and went back to her home. However, not long after, she voiced her displeasure that we took all her money for something she didn't feel she could teach because it didn't meet her standards.

I called her, and I said, "I know you're not happy. What do you want to do? Do you want to teach the class the way it is, or can I offer you a refund?"

She said, "Well, you're just going to give me back my fee for the classes."

I said, "No, you send me a receipt for every penny you paid to be here. I'll pay your hotel. I'll pay your airfare, and I'll give you your fee back. I will give you a 100% refund, if that's what you want, or you can teach the class materials the way you were trained."

She said, "I'll take the refund."

I refunded her everything. I probably lost $3,000 on that deal. But you know what? I slept that night. And I knew that even if she walked around telling people she didn't agree with the course, she could never say she didn't agree with me as a business woman. That's integrity.

Integrity: Food for Thought

➢ List five people who show their integrity in business. What is the character trait you admire the most in each person?

➢ On a scale of 1 to 10 (one being the lowest), rate where you see yourself when it comes to integrity.

➢ Reflect on areas of your life where you feel you can improve your integrity.

➢ In what ways do you show your co-workers, clients, boss, friends and family they are rock stars? If you feel this is something you can improve on? What are three actions you can begin taking this week?

➢ In this chapter I talk about "Happy Money." Do you agree with this concept? Why or why not?

CHAPTER 4

Quiet the Fear and Stand Strong

Spiritual Principle: Self-Support

self-sup·port (noun) the supporting or maintaining of oneself or itself without reliance on outside aid.

There seems to be this idea that to be a successful new business, you need to take out loans, get investors, or even take a second mortgage out on your house in order to start, prove your concept, or to launch. I'd heard of way too many entrepreneurs doing this, only to have the business fail, and they end up in serious debt or worse yet, losing their home or collateral. I was not willing to do that. My plan was to support myself by bootstrapping the business and allow it to grow organically. If it showed that it had merit and was on its way to being a full-blown business, I would get additional capital at that time—doing it smarter, not harder.

We get our money ideas from our childhood, and we perfect them as adults. My mother's mantra about money, which I remember being instilled in me as a kid, was you can never depend on anyone, and you should never take any chances. This whole me against the world mentality does not breed unity, cooperation, or team management, and it is not helpful in starting or growing a successful business. I was not about to let these self-serving thoughts consume me as I started my new company.

Learning Self Support

Growing up, I had to learn to rely on myself at a young age. Not financially, but for my emotional and sometimes even physical needs. Both of my parents were what would be diagnosed today as narcissists. Not being mean here, just stating the truth. Life at home was unpredictable. One minute everything would be fine, and the next, I'd accidentally drop a fork, and my mom would lose it. I never knew what to expect moment to moment, and as a result, today I am able to adapt, pivot, change, and go with the flow. These are great advantages to some not great childhood traumas. I used to sport a t-shirt with pride that said, "Whatever doesn't kill you makes you stronger." Today I do know my parents did the very best they could; however, they were limited people.

My dad did all the cooking in our house, unless he was passed out drunk on the couch, then my brother and I had to fend for ourselves. I remember one time when I was nine-years-old, Dad was out cold, and I could not wake him. We were hungry, but mom wasn't home because she left each evening to study for the LSAT's to get into law school. We didn't know how to cook yet. The cupboards were not bare. I just didn't understand what I could make with what was available. I reached into my dad's pocket while he laid there snoring and took out a five-dollar bill. With that cold hard cash in my hand, I went down the hill to the grocery store to purchase Twinkies and Ho Hos. That evening our dinner was wrapped in silver and plastic packaging.

Early on, I learned to rely on myself because I couldn't rely on the adults in my life. Which is why at 17, right after graduation, I left home and set out on my own. I found a roommate and a job, but I wouldn't say I did a very good job supporting myself. I was more in survival mode, feeling that the world owed me and should support me— whether that was the boss I was working for, the guy I was dating, or the bar I worked in. That led to being dishonest, stealing from them, and not paying my bills. I even "borrowed" money from my parents and didn't pay it back until later in life when I was making amends for all of my wrong doings.

Although I was surviving, I wasn't effectively self-supporting myself. When I decided to stop drinking and drugging, there were people who taught me how to be an adult and less dependent on the world to fix me. That's when I started to learn what self-support meant. I remember having a moment of self-awareness and realizing nobody owed me a damn thing. I had been waiting for everybody to pay me back for what I went through as a kid. It was nobody else's problem. It actually was not even my problem, unless I wanted to keep wallowing in it. It was time to move on and get busy living.

During this pivotal time, I took the rough first 20 years of my life and flipped it with the help of God and my friends. I had to be willing and able to do the necessary work to make the needed changes in my life.

And that's what I did. I became a successful salesperson and supported myself and my daughter for many years until I got sick. All of these experiences shaped me into the person I am today, and they ultimately showed me I am capable of being self-supporting. It doesn't mean I don't ever ask for help from others because I sure do, often. However, it does mean I am confident in my ability to stand on my own two feet and keep going through whatever lies in front of me—such an important skill to have in life and in business.

Self-support showed up when I needed it the most with my Scleroderma. There were so many times I had to walk through hard medical procedures and having this principle at my core made it so much easier for me to stay the course and do what was necessary for the improvement of my health. Whether that was inside the MRI machine or CT Scan, or lying awake on an operating table as I watched on a monitor a catheter tube being threaded into my neck, reaching all the way to my heart for the 3rd time, I needed to rely on myself to get through it.

With my company, self-support means not writing checks with my mouth that the company bank balance can't cash. We stay within our means and strive to keep going. A slow but steady rise in business and partner clients has taken us to the much desired one-million dollar in booked business sales mark in 2017. Staying cash flow positive in the black for years now with no debt and enviable accounts receivable is all a direct result of me, as the CEO, taking a strong look at what we absolutely must have and what can we do without.

When it comes to my employees, I have learned so much from my mentors. They have taught me to think outside the box when I am considering hiring a new employee. It is good to step back and think about whether or not I need to bring on a full-time employee. Could I get a part-time consultant to do the job without the heavy burden of another salary? Are there tasks other staff members could pick up and manage? Taking the time to think through the options, without rushing to make a decision, has been a key ingredient to the success of the company.

As an added incentive to my full-time staff, I have added profit sharing. This great benefit allows everyone to share in the success and positive results from all their hard work. They understand that at times they may have extra tasks to take care of, but they know they will be rewarded for their time and effort. Since we are self-supporting, we are also able to be self-sharing.

Quieting That 2 AM Voice

That being said, building a successful business goes beyond the financials. A key element of creating a self-supporting company is the ability to be able to calm those negative voices in your head. It's hard to not let doubt and insecurities consume you when you are taking a risk and starting something new.

I believe we all have a negative voice in our head that will shove its way to the front, if we are not careful. We can imagine it to be that of a parent, a teacher, boss, ex-husband, our own voice, or for me, it can be a mashup of all of these. It tells us we are not good enough, smart enough, strong enough, creative enough and gets us questioning many different areas of our lives and the decisions we are making, but not in a positive way. For me it was very present the first few years of the business.

Thanks to my Scleroderma, I am used to telling that voice to quiet down because if I had listened to those negative, sad, Debbie Downer messages it was sending, I believe I would be dead. Simple as that. Give in to doubt and die.

For me, it happens in the middle of the night. I call it my 2 AM voice, and it fills my head with negative thoughts, doubt, and fear. It tries to consume me, and I have to work hard at pushing it away. It reminds me of a Native American legend I have heard many times since my illness began:

One evening, an old Cherokee told his grandson about a battle that goes on inside people. He said, "My son, the battle is between two wolves inside us all. One is Evil—it is anger, envy, jealousy, sorrow, regret, greed, arrogance, self-pity, guilt, resentment, inferiority, lies, false pride, superiority, and ego. The other is Good—it is joy, peace, love, hope, serenity, humility, kindness, benevolence, empathy, generosity, truth, compassion, and faith." The grandson thought about it for a minute and then asked his grandfather, "Which wolf wins?" The old Cherokee simply replied, "The one you feed."

My goal is to not feed that negative 2 AM voice in my head.

I've had to work hard to discern whether that voice was reality or fear. In the still quiet of the dark, it torments me, but in the daylight, I can handle it.

When I first started the business, that voice came in strong, saying things like:

Oh my God, what did I do?

I'm never going to get anywhere with this business. Do I really think I can change this industry?

Nobody wants to provide nutrition information on their menus.

I'm going to bankrupt myself and my family.

Nobody cares about allergies.

This is the craziest damn thing in the world!

I had to mentally step back and put those thoughts through a filter and shift the perspective to:

Menu labeling is a needed service.

I have more courage than that man who runs a billion-dollar business. He said so.

Why not me? I can be the one to do this as much as anyone else can.

This great team, and I can make this happen.

Helping people with this business is my true passion.

Empowering statements like these help me drown out the ones that say, *What in God's name were you thinking?* That negative voice still wakes me up, but the stronger I become, the less time I spend listening to it. I realize it's not based on truth, and I recognize it for what it is: FEAR (false evidence appearing real). And then I replace it with a clearer, more positive voice.

The benefit of having a fatal progressive illness like scleroderma is I get to measure everything against the fact that I didn't die. Not all decisions I make and ventures I try will have a good outcome, but I know that if I fail at something, I will get back up and keep going. After all, I have faced death, and I am still alive. Nothing will hold me back. A failed business or new product line within the company is small potatoes compared to dying. It puts everything in a real simple, but clear, perspective

2 AM Friends

Sometimes, no matter what I do, that voice takes me hostage. I have a few people in my life who I can count on to help me, day or night. They are my 2 AM friends. When that voice is screaming, and I can't get away from the fear, they are there for me. Have I picked the phone up, texted, or Facebook messaged them in the middle of the night? Hell, yes!

I have been blessed with great folks surrounding me since I was a young adult and was ready to accept help. In my 20s, these friends helped me stop drinking, get stable, and begin to be a mom. They taught me how to function in life, as I like to say, on life's terms. When my daughter was brand new, and I was losing my mind because I didn't know how to be a mom, and she had been crying for hours, they helped. Then in my 40s, I got sick and felt like I was going to die. They reminded me I was too damn stubborn and strong to die right now. They helped me process through that fear, that mental back and forth that made me nuts at two in the morning.

These friends have saved me from myself many times, and I am grateful. I pay it forward whenever I can by leaving my phone on and being available at all hours of the night for anyone who needs me. I understand how debilitating that negative voice can be, and I want to help others work through that, regardless of what time it is.

Getting Help

Part of self-support comes from being thoughtful about the people I surround myself with while staying true to myself. Who am I listening to, and what do I want the future to look like? A large number of folks have wanted to jump on and hitch their wagon to mine because my company is new and exhilarating and doing something super forward- thinking in an exciting and popular industry. That's all fine and dandy, but do they have qualities I want to see grow within my business? Do they represent my values and the company culture I am trying to build and foster?

When I first started the university/college AllerTrain™ U training side of the business, I kept running into one company's name over and over. So, I did what any confident, strong-willed CEO does, I looked up the CEO of that company and connected with him on LinkedIN. He accepted my connection in a matter of minutes, even though it was a Saturday afternoon. I turned around and sent him an email, telling him I wanted to speak with him and asked him if he could spare some time. This amazing leader said, "Sure, call me Monday at 9 AM EST," and then went on to give me his direct phone line.

Over the weekend, I made the mistake of looking up the details on him, his company, and what he did on a daily basis. Let me just say I was overwhelmed by his amazing credentials and experience as he managed a business that had annual revenues in the billions. But I wasn't going to let that stop me, so at 9 AM sharp on Monday, I called him. I had a list of questions he was gracious enough to answer, and we had a great conversation. Over time we became friends. He has helped me with ideas and has answered my questions on more than one occasion. At one point, this CEO told me what I was doing took more guts then he ever had. This line is one I have repeated when I needed it, at all different points in my company's growth.

Sometimes the wrong kind of help shows up, and you have to be strong enough to move on and trust that the right kind of help is out there. Early on when I got sick, I had a rheumatologist who, every single time I saw him, kept adding more and more medicine to my already full cocktail of drugs. His vision was to throw meds at every symptom, and mine was to get off the meds and end up taking as little as possible. I treated certain symptoms without meds at all, if possible. Meditation, yoga, and long baths helped increase movement of my arms and legs when meds didn't or couldn't do anything more. In the spirit of self-support, you know what I did? I fired that Doc. I moved on and found a great doctor who was willing to try new things, and when he ran out of options, then he sent me to the Scleroderma Clinic in Denver. When we reach out for help, we need to find those whose vision aligns with ours. Covering up all my symptoms with more medication was not what I wanted for my life, so I had to take it upon myself to do something about it.

Not all help is good, and we need to be aware and willing to move on if necessary.

Being the Expert

During the early years, I realized that to grow our company, I needed to implement some PR and marketing. I could spend tens of thousands of dollars to hire a big sales and marketing firm. This would mean getting outside money, like a line of credit, to fund it. I didn't want to do that. I needed to work out a more self-supporting option to spread the word about my brand-new baby company I loved so much and get people to listen.

I read the book, *The Millionaire Messenger*, by Brendon Buchard. It shared the importance of becoming a subject matter expert on a topic, how to become the expert, and then how to share that message and expertise. This was the perfect solution for me. If all the lights dimmed down, and the only light was on me in the front of the room sharing my information, they would listen. They would know my name and my message.

The book was a step-by-step guide. It came from this idea that anybody could be a subject matter expert on any topic, if they were willing to do the simple tasks lined out in the book. Things like research the topic, take classes, dealing with outside criticism as a way to improve, and doing a self-inventory on your feelings about speaking in front of a group. In my mind, it was the equivalent to years of Toastmasters all squeezed into a book.

I was ready to do the work needed to become an expert. But because my topic was so innovative at the time, there wasn't anybody out there teaching menu-labeling. There were few resources. My best source was the FDA. For months, I visited their website daily, reading and soaking up all the information I could. Soon after Obama signed the Affordable Health Care

Act, and section 4205 regarding menu labeling was in there, the FDA opened up their website to public comment. This was great for me. I could watch what the public, restaurant owners, and consultants were saying about menu-labeling, and it was all there, free, for me to look at. I became addicted to learning all I could about this topic and understanding how people felt about it.

Also, there was a lobbying group in DC that was on the cutting- edge of menu labeling, and they turned out to be an abundant source of information. I made it my business to meet the woman credited with getting the first menu labeling laws passed in regions, well in advance of the federal (national) law.

Since another goal was to speak to groups, I wanted to make sure I became as effective as possible when I stood in the front of the room talking about nutrition and food allergies. I am a classic Type A, East Coast personality. So, for me to slow down and be gentler when I talk was a challenge. When I get excited, it's like a bullet train coming out of the station—fast, direct, and loud with very few periods at the end of my sentences.

I had to learn how to be a better speaker in order to get my message across clearer. Being self-supporting, I went online to look for help and options. The founder of Ted Talks has a whole video series on how to be an effective speaker. It took me less than ten hours to view those. Then I watched other Ted Talks. I'd pay attention to how the person spoke and not so much what they were saying—focusing on their inflection and tone. I'd watch what they did with their hands, how fast they spoke, and how much they moved on stage. Pulling from my early experiences as a DJ, I also knew how to make people laugh and entertain them. I incorporated all those skills and techniques into my own talks to strengthen my presence as the subject matter expert.

Armed with my topic, my new speaking skills, and my desire to be the expert in this uncharted area in the hospitality industry, I went to any place that would let me run my mouth about those topics. The first big presentation I gave in front of C-level executives was the Fast Casual Executive Summit. I shared my knowledge, and when asked tough questions, I did not back down because I knew what I was talking about.

What was cool about that experience was that it led to other opportunities. The next year I got invited to speak at three different state conferences. I still speak at these each year and share the latest trends and hot topics regarding food labeling and allergies. It markets our business like nothing I've ever seen. People will hear me, or they'll hear about me, or they come talk to me, and that's where many of our clients come from.

I am now the subject matter expert, and big companies want to partner with subject matter experts. It has allowed me to become the "IBM" of the menu labeling and food allergies. I don't think there is a better way to market a business than to stand up front and wow people with knowledge—to take detailed, complicated information, make it bite-sized and manageable, and deliver it with total confidence.

I invested that time and energy into being the expert that other companies sought. My initial motivation was not wanting to cash in one more 401(k) or max out one more credit card. It was more feasible for me to spend $1,000 to drive to events, spend the night in an inexpensive hotel, and wear my best Ann Taylor dress that I bought off a clearance rack, than to pay for an outside agency. Being the expert allowed me to expand the business and continue to be self-supportive.

Don't Hold On, Give It Away

Something that goes along with being the subject matter expert is to share your knowledge and wisdom. You want to be known as the go-to person in your industry, and one of the best ways to do that is be the one others come to for information and advice. For me, when someone thinks about menu labeling and food allergy safety, I want my name to be one of the first ones that comes to mind. I can do that by sharing what I know.

Most months, my company does a free webinar. We give continuing education credits, which brings great value to those who take the webinars. Our blog, *Pick Your Poison*, shares the weird chemicals and ingredients in certain foods. On the Allergen side of the house, we are always providing the latest and greatest information to those in the food industry. As a company, we give that information away with a huge smile.

Recently, there has been a lot of legislation that impacts the restaurant industry. This has some restauranteurs scared because they don't have all the information they need, and they are unsure where to find it. In order to continue being the subject-matter expert in this space, I have stayed current on the latest laws. I then share what I know with those who want to know more in order to arm them with knowledge

I just did a webinar a week ago on new laws for food allergies across the country. Illinois just passed one for their entire state that was to go into effect in 60 days. The law was passed, the state restaurant association got the news, and no one knew it was coming.

To help ease their fears, I did a webinar explaining all the different laws mandated across the US. It was 30 minutes. I footed the bill, then put it up on our YouTube channel for anyone to watch. Ultimately, it will bring me clients because our training class meets those mandates. But the main reason behind the video is that every time someone watches it, it brings goodwill. It brings the fellowship of sharing information and the expertise to their door.

You Don't Always Have to Ride Solo

This concept of relying on yourself in your business is helpful, but there are times when this can be a detriment more than a benefit. Self-support has worked against me in business, during those times when I play Lone Ranger. I jump on my horse, hands in the air, and yell, "I got this!"

When I first started the business, I knew I needed a website. Rocky was busy with his full-time job and making sure the software he created for the company worked efficiently, so he didn't have the time to build the whole site. I could hire someone, but I didn't have the money at the time to do so.

Time to saddle up the horse and learn how to do it myself. "Hi-Yo Silver, away!" My plan was to create an amazing website. Rocky created the basic backend, but I was determined to do the rest myself. There was a local Meetup group that focused on creating websites. I went to the meetings to learn all I could. I'd go there and listen to them and then go home and try it.

Then I bought a book, *WordPress 101.* I set aside a Saturday to go through the book chapter by chapter and try things as I went along. I learned basic design techniques, how to insert photos, how to make a contact form, format text...everything I needed to make an amazing website.

I spent eight hours in our basement putting it all together, barely even getting up to go to the bathroom. At the end of the day, I had a 31-page website. it was probably twice big as it needed to be, but I felt proud of my accomplishment. I was excited to show Rocky. Before I went upstairs, I hit a button, and the whole thing disappeared. I stared at the blank screen, then completely lost my mind.

Rage surged through me as I stomped up the stairs. Rocky sat on his red recliner and looked up at me as I emerged from the basement. This was completely my fault, but I had no intention of standing in front of the mirror yelling at myself. Rocky became my lightening rod, and I directed all my fury at him.

"Why didn't you tell me I needed to back up the website? Why didn't you tell me to save my progress along the way?"

He sat there and looked at me, not saying a word, so I continued. "You are the technical side of the company. Why did you let me think I could do the website? What were you thinking? Now there is no website! It's gone! You should have been there with me! You should have helped me!"

He continued to stare at me, no reaction on his face (thank goodness one of us can remain calm).

"Don't you have anything to say!" I yelled.

Nothing.

"I'm out of here!" I stormed out of the house, got in my car, and I drove. Obscenities flowed out of my mouth like a raging river as I headed toward a great hiding place for me when I get overwhelmed, the movies.

About an hour later I texted Rocky, "I just want to let you know I am safe. I am sitting in the movie theater, and I hate everything right now. I should have never started this company. I don't even want to talk right now. I'll be home later."

He responded, "I love you, and I can't wait to see you."

As I watched *Under the Tuscan Sun* and escaped into the beautiful Italian scenery and the story, I realized how lucky I was to have such an amazing partner in marriage and in life. He could have easily (and understandably) yelled back at me and told me to get on my broom and fly out of there. But he didn't. He let me vent and get it out of my system.

Rather than ask for assistance along the way, I went bull-headed into eight hours of development on my own and crashed my website. I was too headstrong to reach out, and it nearly cost me my business because I was ready to give up right there.

When I got home, Rocky looked at me, smiled, and said, "Go check your website."

I ran downstairs, and there on the screen was my beautiful site. He was able to save all but the last 30 minutes of changes I had done. Happiness and gratefulness all washed over me, and I let out a huge sigh of relief.

I went upstairs and hugged him. "Thank you. Thank you for always being here for me and for putting up with my craziness. I am one lucky woman."

Even though I thought I could *Lone Ranger* it and do the whole website on my own, I should have paused along the way to find the experts and ask their advice. Rocky would have gladly done this, but he knows me well enough to understand that when I decide to do something on my own, it's best he leave me alone to do it.

Today, I still work on the website and do about 70% of the updates and changes. But I have two experts on retainer that I can reach out to anytime with questions or to have them take care of items that might be more than I can handle. I may be stubborn and bull-headed, but I am a quick learner.

In business, while self-support is an amazing quality to have, there are times when it is necessary to reach out for assistance. It could be because we aren't knowledgeable enough to do something on our own, or maybe our time would be spent better doing something else. Regardless of the reason, it is ok to enlist a sidekick and not always ride solo.

Self-Support: Food for Thought

➤ Think back to your childhood. In what ways were you taught to be self-supportive? How has that carried into your life today?

➤ Early in the chapter, I talk about the 2 AM voice trying to fill our heads with negative thoughts and fears. Make a list of three recurring thoughts you have. Now, take those negative thoughts and write three positive ones. Cross off the negative list and re-read the positive list a few times.

➤ Who are your 2 AM friends? Reflect on all the ways they support you in your business and personal life. Have you let them know lately how much you appreciate them?

➤ What are you currently or hope to be a subject matter expert in for your job? List three steps you can take to become even more knowledgeable in this area.

Asking for Help: A Strength, Not a Weakness

Spiritual Principle: Ask for Help

help (verb) to give or provide what is necessary to accomplish a task or satisfy a need; contribute strength or means to render assistance to; to relieve (someone) in need, sickness, pain, or distress

A sking for help at 20 years old saved my life. It taught me how to put down alcohol and pick up a whole new life I never dreamed was possible for me. Desperation had taken a hold of me and asking for help felt like my only option. It wasn't an easy principle to learn at the time, but it helped me grow and realize that asking for help is not a sign of weakness, but one of strength. It can take a lot of courage to reach out and trust others. But I have found when I am brave, I am rewarded with the kindness of others.

Mentors have played a huge role in my life, both personally and in business. Back in 1985, I needed someone to teach me the ropes of how to live a life without alcohol and drugs—how to stay away from drinking and make better choices in all areas of my life. Even today, I still today have a mentor I speak with regularly in my personal life who helps me do the right thing and stay on track. But I also have other mentors. Recently, they have been much more of a business variety—people who understand the life of an entrepreneur, marketing, growth, and how to run a successful company. They are there to support me in all my business affairs. Today all of these rock stars are equally valuable in my life for sure.

Between 20 and 40 years old, asking for help from a higher power became a daily practice for me. Having a strong spiritual belief during these years was essential to my life as my core beliefs shifted. Spiritually, asking for help from a higher power is simply praying. Receiving that help is meditation and listening. Back then, I started the daily practice of prayer and meditation, and I continue it today. The messages and thoughts received are astounding.

In addition to asking for help, it is important to be a gracious receiver of it and to be courteous and give help when asked. When others in the industry ask for my assistance, I am happy to oblige. And because they know me, they know it will get done and with a smile on my face. It's a business reputation that's worth more than any amount of money you could put in a bank. It's not a capital you trade at the cash register, but it's capital that people understand; if they ask you to do something and you are there, the value of this is priceless.

Windows and doors of opportunity don't open without that wiling spirit of asking for help, receiving help, and giving help.

Receiving Help

Right around the time I turned 21, my prior, out-of-control life was catching up to me. I was finally living without alcohol, but my life was in chaos. During all those crazy times, my biggest concern was making enough money to keep me supplied with drugs and alcohol. Paying bills and saving money were not high on my list of things to do, in fact, they hardly made the list at all. Then I found myself broke and about to be evicted from my friend's condo. Living my life fully engaged and sober was turning out to be harder than I imagined. When I stopped dancing long enough for everything to catch up, it did.

I went to meet some friends one evening, and it must have been clear from my facial expression that something was wrong.

My friend, Tom, came up to me, "What has you so upset?"

"I'm sick and don't feel well. My doctor prescribed an antibiotic, but I just don't have the 40 bucks to pay for it. Don't worry, Bud, I'll figure it out." I tried to keep the frustrated tears at bay.

"That's tough. Sorry to hear that." He put his arm around my shoulder.

Later when everyone was leaving, Tom said, "Hey, you got a sec?"

"Sure."

"Take a ride with me?"

"Where are we going?" I asked.

"To that pharmacy," he replied.

I knew it! My head spun not knowing what the right thing was for me to do. I was almost 21 years old and couldn't even afford a med for 40 bucks? That was a hard pill to swallow. Should I deal with it and live without the meds, or let this man buy them for me?

The pharmacist at the drug store recognized me from being in there earlier when I tried to get the medication. He smiled and grabbed it for me as I approached with Tom.

Tom stepped up and laid down two twenty-dollar bills, and off we went.

"Thank you." Emotion overwhelmed me, and I hugged him extra hard so he would know how much I appreciated it.

I hadn't asked for help, but I was grateful he recognized my desperation and stepped in, whether I wanted him to or not.

We are still friends today, 30+ years later.

I said to him once, about five years after the incident, "I really need to pay you back for that prescription."

He said, "No, I want you to pay it forward."

And that is exactly what I have done with different folks over the years because I remember his kindness and how much that helped me.

There is a great lesson here about being a gracious receiver of help. For me, it is not always easy. I don't want to be seen as weak or incapable of taking care of myself. It is a matter of letting the ego go. But over the years, I have learned the importance of allowing others to be of service to me and accept it with a smile and a thank you. This has served me well in my personal life and in my business.

A Little Help from My Friends

As I mentioned before, my dad stopped drinking in 1984 for the first time, and I saw the positive impact it had on his life. If a man who was not often there for me could seek help, I wondered if it would work for me as well? Turning to strangers to ask for help was one of the hardest things I ever had to do; however, I knew I couldn't function on my own without alcohol, and I knew it was killing me a day at a time.

Once I initially reached out for support with my drinking, it became easier to ask for help if it related to that issue. But when it came to other areas in my life, like being sick, I relied on myself and my husband. I refused to reach out to others.

I remember the day I finally asked for help. My friend, Jay, remembers it as the day I finally *allowed* him to help. I laid in bed watching Rocky carefully arrange my supplies for the day on the nightstand next to the bed.

"Ok, Babe, you have everything you need here," he said. "There is food, water, and your medications. Is there anything else you need before I leave?"

I smiled, "No. You are amazing. Go enjoy your day, and don't worry about me. I'll be fine."

He gently kissed me, "I love you."

"I love you too."

I watched him leave and thought about how lucky I was to have such a wonderful husband. He never intended to be my full-time caregiver, but that's where he ended up. He became the best nurse any engineer ever was. When my scleroderma got to the point where I had to stay confined to my bed or the couch for the majority of the day, he was there. He worked from home most days in order to take care of me. He had to dress me, help me bathe, and wash lots of sheets. He helped me track my medication, brought me food, and comforted me when the intense pain wracked my body and all I could do was scream and cry. He did all this with love and kindness. Rocky was a saint.

But even saints need a break, and today was that day for him. He felt drained, and we both knew that if he didn't take some time to recharge, he was going to crash and burn. I heard the garage door close and the car go down the road. I settled in, turned on the television, and focused my attention on something else besides the pain coursing through my body.

A couple hours of later, I reached for my Oxycodone. The pills were for the excruciating breakthrough pain that came on top of the two morphine patches I had on me 24/7. I am generally a tough cookie, and even during my drugging days, I never took downers like opioids. But now, these meds helped me survive the agony each day and were a necessity.

Panic surged through me. I had enough for one more dose, but it was not enough to get me through the rest of the day. Rocky wasn't going to be home until the evening. Imagining the intensity of the pain that would consume my body once the medication wore off scared the hell out of me.

Thoughts raced through my head.

I could try to go get it myself, but who was I kidding. That wasn't possible.

I could call Rocky, but he needed this day to himself.

I could suffer through the pain.

Or I could reach out to a friend.

I didn't want to burden anyone else with my problems. But as I laid there, I knew I needed to do something.

My hands shook as I held back the tears and called my friend.

"Jay, this is Betsy. I need your help."

"Of course," he said. "Whatever you need, Hun. I'm here for you."

"Rocky's had it and is out enjoying a day to himself, so I don't want to bother him. And I really hate having to ask you to do this."

"Bets, as I've told you before, I am always here for you. So, what do you need?"

"I need a refill on my pain meds. Can you go pick those up for me?"

"Absolutely. I will leave now and be there as soon as I can."

"Thank you, Jay. This means a lot to me. When you get here, come on up, I am in my bedroom."

I gave him the information about how and where to get my prescription. As I waited for him, anxiety crept in. I wondered if he was actually going to do this for me.

Growing up, my parents stayed focused on themselves and were unreliable when my brother or I asked for help, but they were amazingly helpful to their friends or strangers. We could never count on them to say yes, or if they did, there was no guarantee they would follow through. It was just how things went at home. As I got older, this idea that you can't always count on people remained ingrained in me. Even when people offered to help, I always held on to this lingering doubt that they might not follow through. This situation was no different. Jay had never given me a reason not to trust him, but that doubt sat in the shadows.

Plus, I did not want him to see me like this, lying in my bed in my nightgown, hair matted to my head, and doing everything I could to manage the horrible pain that consumed my body. I felt extremely vulnerable. It was one thing for Rocky to see me like this, but not someone else, even if that someone else happened to be a good friend.

When Jay arrived, he was sweet and kind like always. I wanted to cry. He put the meds on the nightstand and asked if I needed anything else. I told him I would be fine now and how much I appreciated him.

He looked me in the eyes and said, "I am always available to help. You just need to ask."

"Thank you," I told him. "You are a dear friend."

"Call if you need anything else. Ok?"

"Ok," I said. "I will."

And I did. Not that same day, but I did. But on that day, I learned that I can't do everything by myself, and I didn't need to rely solely on my husband to take care of me. There were others in my life, waiting to step in, but they needed me to ask.

Following that day, Jay or his wife checked in on me periodically through text or a phone call to ask if I needed anything. One time, I told him I really wanted root beer popsicles because it helped with the nausea caused by medications. He brought some right over. Another time, he and his wife brought me dinner. I can still see the smile on Jay's wife's face as she walked into the house, dinner in hand to feed me and my family. So kind and much appreciated.

Asking for help is not a sign of weakness. It actually shows strength. Trusting those in your life, whether at work or at home, to give you support takes courage. But in the end, it builds deeper connections and allows others to be of service to you.

It Doesn't Hurt to Ask

Asking for help advances your business. I have seen this play out many times for me with my company. Right after I started the business, I wanted to do a press release announcing the opening of the business. I found an article in a leading trade magazine that quoted the founder of Healthy Dining Finder (a big competitor at that time). I reached out to her and asked her if I could use her quotes in my press release. I wanted to give it more weight by having an expert quote from someone already well known in the field.

"You want to use my words?" she asked. "No problem."

It was super cool. I just asked my number one competitor to help me, and she said yes.

It's where I took the philosophy of asking for help that I learned when I stopped drinking, and I knew it could work in business. Fast forward that to today—I have been on the phone with these same folks, talking about how we might work side by side moving forward to better the entire industry.

I don't see people as competition. They might have a competing product, but that's okay. I don't actually care. I don't have to shy away from them as people, and I can be nice to them. I can learn their names, eat dinner with them, wish them happy birthday, and be Facebook friends. There is nothing that says I can't do any of that (and even if there was, it still wouldn't matter to me). These connections have been amazing because when I need help, advice, or insight into the industry, they are happy to help even though I am their competition.

I remember going to a tradeshow in California where other companies that provided nutritional information for food service were also seeking new clients for menu labeling. One competitor had her booth a few aisles away. I was busy setting mine up with beautiful floor plants I had bought. My plan was to create a welcoming space to lure people toward ours. I needed to hang something up and realized I didn't have what I needed.

I went over her booth, "I forgot to bring my scissors and tape. Do you have some I can borrow?"

"Of course, Betsy, no problem."

At the end of the show I had these plants. I knew the airline would not be thrilled if I tried to take them on the plane, but I didn't want to throw them out. I took them over to this woman's booth because she lived in the area.

"Thanks for sharing your supplies with me," I said. "I would like you have these. I can't take them with me."

"Really?" she said. "Those are beautiful. It was just scissors and tape."

"Sure, but it was something I needed, and you were willing to help," I said. "That means a lot to me, and these are a way to say thank you."

"That's so nice of you," she smiled. "I appreciate it, and I have the perfect place to put them."

This wasn't about two competing businesses; this was about two businesswomen, helping and supporting each other. I hear all the time how women don't support women. My experience has been the exact opposite.

My 2 AM friend, Kathleen, taught me a great concept the year I started my company. We were both at a trade show, and she gave a presentation. During it she said, "If you want to be a millionaire, hang out with millionaires." The idea being, if I want to be at that level, I needed to associate with people who are already there and learn from them. I took this advice to heart and began paying more attention to my major competitors.

By aiming high, I can catch a star. If all I aim for is the low hanging fruit, that's all I will get. I can't expect to achieve the level of success I strive for if I stay in my comfort zone. I must reach higher. I call it "dating up." I pay attention to and seek advice from those who may initially appear to be "out of my league." People tend to be intimated and scared off by the CEOs of companies. All they see is the money and prestige and assume they don't have time for those "beneath them." This has not been the case for me. I have found they will go to lunch with me just as easily as anyone else. They have been gracious in sharing their knowledge and experiences with me; all I had to do was ask.

Give it away to keep it is a spiritual teaching of when I help you improve your life, my life is blessed twice. This is a concept that made me whole again in my 20s, so I wanted to apply it to the business and see if it worked there.

What I discovered is everybody wants to pass it on. Whether it's a hobby like fly fishing or how to run a successful company, people get joy in passing on what they are passionate about.

Can I Help You?

One of the things I set out to do in 2010 was be the solution for the nutrition needs of the restaurant industry. We are now that solution. For our clients who pay us monthly for our services, we are their nutrition help desk. They call us with a variety of questions, like is there egg or soy in the pizza crust from a certain restaurant. Our job is to find that out for clients, so they can answer that question for their consumers. We do it with certainty, confidence, and a smile in our answer, so the client and the consumer can trust what we say.

Because we are known as a nutrition company, when one of our clients is trying a new diet or is having a reaction from a food, many times they will call us to talk about it. It has nothing to do with the contract they have with us, but they need to talk with someone. They will ask our opinion and get our take on it. We have become valued and trusted in the area of nutrition.

Recently, a good friend of mine, who is also a client, needed to go on a wicked, restricted diet for three weeks before a procedure. She travels constantly and wanted to know some options for food while she was on the road. One of my employees figured out what she could eat at places like Starbucks and Panera, even with the new restricted diet. My friend now knew that when she went to Starbucks, she could get a green tea, one of their new bento boxes, throw 2 items from the box away, and she could eat everything else. Sure, she could have gotten that information from a dietician, but her appointment was still two weeks out. She needed that information quickly from someone she trusted.

Providing these answers isn't technically part of the contract we hold with clients, but it is part of a much more powerful contract. The spiritual contract of helping and being of service. Always, no matter what. It's what I do personally, and now, what we do as a company every chance we get.

I am very appreciative when people sense I need help. Like when I needed antibiotics, Tom bought them for me, and I didn't even have to ask. I think it is kind, and I try to do that with others whenever possible as a way to pay it forward.

Recently, I was on the phone with a client who has multiple restaurant locations throughout the world. He was telling me about a food allergy training he was getting ready to do in Illinois. As a way to give back to the community, he and his company planned to give away 250 orange backpacks filled with food to lower income kids who didn't always get three meals a day. The issue was, he was having trouble filling the backpacks.

I said to him, "OK, honestly, why can't you get food? You are one of the biggest food service companies in the world. What's the problem?"

"Long story, but we can't get it from our normal sources for this project," he said.

I saw this as an opening to do for others and give some help in an instant.

"Can I sponsor the food for that?"

"Really?" he asked.

"Yes. Can I send you a check and have your people go buy the food for the backpacks?"

He was so overwhelmed, "Betsy, you really want to do that?"

"Of course, yes. I want to do it so bad I can't see straight."

"Thank you! I will have someone from corporate get in touch with you." I sent the money. I also included a check from my personal account, and they filled the backpacks with food. This client didn't ask for help. He assumed he could do it on his own. I wasn't seeking sponsorship opportunities to help market my company. This was him sharing a challenge he was experiencing and me being open to offer him assistance when I saw a need I could fill.

Allowing people to help me has made me more vulnerable than I've ever been in my life. Reaching out to Jay was that first step in better understanding the importance of asking for help. It scared me some, and still scares me a little. But in the end, it has made me a much stronger woman. I've been able to pivot that into becoming a strong business woman, a strong business owner, and a strong leader in this industry.

I have an office full of people who I appreciate and who appreciate me. I have successful colleagues in the industry who are willing to share their knowledge and expertise with me. I have mentors taking time to ensure my company is on track. It's all too big for me to do alone anymore, and I am grateful there are people in my life ready to provide the help and support I need to make the business successful.

If I am going to ask for help, then I better be willing to do my part to follow through and do the work that needs to be done. I believe there are people out there that ask for help, so they don't have to do the work. They want the easy way out. I don't agree with that. I have a responsibility to do my part and follow through to the best of my ability if I am asking someone else to go out on a limb for me. It's a give and take.

Ask for Help: Food for Thought

➢ On a scale of 1 to 10 (one being the lowest), rate yourself on your ability to **receive** help. Is this something you can improve on? If so, what are the steps you will take to do that?

➢ On a scale of 1 to 10 (one being the lowest), rate yourself on your ability to **give** help. Is this something you can improve on? If so, what are the steps you will take to do that?

➢ Reflect on a time at work when you had to ask for help. What was the result?

➢ What are four ways you are helpful to others at work? At home?

➢ List three rock stars in your line of work that you would love to connect with. Reflect on what makes them so amazing. Choose one to reach out to.

CHAPTER 6

Don't Quit…Pivot

Spiritual Principle: Persistence

per·sist·ence (noun) firm or obstinate continuance in a course of action in spite of difficulty or opposition.

To me, the principle of persistence equates to being unstoppable. It's about facing challenges head on and not giving up until you have succeeded or tried every avenue possible, and once you have tried everything possible, you dig a little deeper and try just a few more things. When I was a kid, I survived my very challenging, but for many, a typical childhood, because I saw glimpses of a better life in those around me. Knowing if I stuck it out, I could have a future that was better for me kept me going through very tough times as a kid.

After running wild with my drinking until 20, and then quitting alcohol to change pretty much every aspect of my life, I was on fire, determined to prove to the world and myself that I could be a success. Success for me at 20 looked very simple— lots of money and flash. A friend of mine explained it best when she said that I used people and acquired things. Money and the balance in my accounts determined my worth or lack thereof.

It was a very self-willed, full speed ahead, self-centered time for me. Scleroderma was the one thing that stopped me in my tracks.

Getting a death sentence at 41 years old shook me to the core, and I wasn't sure I could push through the diagnosis and the take my breath away levels of pain. But with God's help, and a little grit, I dug deep to a level within even I didn't know I possessed and found that fighting spirit wrapped around the God-given strength to keep going. Once I was able to go back to school, and then eventually back to work, hope filled me like never before. I became more determined, knowing this was my only true choice.

What Really Matters

When you grow up with multiple layers of insanity in your home, you learn to present a different face to the world—one that gives the illusion that everything is fine. You wear masks to hide behind when needed. Then you figure out how to get people on your side through whatever means possible. It is a much-needed survival skill that, I must say, I perfected and not always in a positive way.

In my 20s, I shifted from the nightlife of the bar business to a day job in sales, to the restaurant business. With my binder of products to sell and an order pad to fill out, off I went. I soon found I had a strong and true gift for it. At that time, sales meant persuading, and even at times manipulating people into buying something from me. The more persistent I was, the more success I experienced; and I was very successful.

During these early years of my career, it was all about making a lot of money and having nice things in life. Even though I grew up on the right side of the tracks, I seemed to have an unquenchable thirst for more. Always more. It didn't matter what I was trying to acquire; food, clothes, and in my younger years, alcohol, the answer was always the same. During recovery, we often ask, "What was your favorite drink or drug?" My answer has always been "more." Guess it is deep within my DNA.

When I was old enough, I used money and material possessions to fill a void in my heart or a sickness in my soul. I would make a sale and then go into Nordstrom's and find a pair of shoes I liked and buy them in five colors, because I could. Then I would get a Coach purse to match. I believed this was the key to happiness and nothing could stop me. But all the money in the world wasn't going to give me what I always craved—those true gifts in life that make it worth living, gifts like love, contentment, security, faith, and peace.

I now own a million-dollar business, but today my view of what constitutes success is drastically different from what it used to be, thanks to my Scleroderma. While laying on that couch, I was blessed with a lot of time to reflect on where I had come from, what was currently in my life, and where I wanted to go. What was important? My health, physical, mental, and spiritual? Or a bunch of shoes from a fancy department store? I realized it was going to take faith like I could hardly imagine and a lot of follow through to change the path I was on prior to getting sick. Being confined to the couch for so long brought me to place where I could better understand what really mattered. In a very crazy way, and even though I NEVER thought I would say it, I am thankful for scleroderma and all It has taught me. If I hadn't gotten sick, I wouldn't have had my moment of truth, my come to Jesus talk with myself.

Do I still want to make money? You bet, but now it goes beyond the money. There's a saying I learned when I stopped drinking and drugging, "You've got to give it away to keep it." The spiritual law works this way for me: If I worry about your plate being full of food, then for some crazy reason, I find that

I am not hungry. My focus is not self-centered like it was in the past. It has nothing to do with filling my closet with new, expensive clothes, shoes, and more things. What's important to me now is having a positive impact on the restaurant industry and being the voice for those with food allergies. My mission, and that of my company, is to protect lives and health through nutrition and training. Yup, that's what I do on a daily basis.

I wanted to take that same drive and persistence I used in my young adult years to stop drinking, wrapped around that the principles I learned from many great folks, and apply all of that to a business. My goal was to make it authentic. That's what I did with MenuTrinfo®. I stopped looking at sales and money as a way to become wealthy, and instead, I created a company that values its clients, employees, and strives to make the world a better place.

Time to Pivot

In 2008, the world was hit with the worst global financial crisis since the Great Depression. By 2010, the banks began to stabilize, but people remained cautious. I stayed optimistic and believed I could start a successful business, regardless of what the country had experienced in its economic markets. I can't even begin to tell you how many people told me not to start a new business, especially one that had never been done before. On the flip side, here were also those who told me to go for it. Especially anyone who understood firsthand about diet, nutrition, food allergies, and food being medicine. They jumped on the bandwagon and started to be my cheerleaders from day one. Interestingly enough, many on both the pro and the con side thought I needed a Master's in Public Health or at least an undergrad degree in nutrition or food science. Even with this opposition, I continued to be confident. I knew deep down in my gut I could make this work.

When Obama signed the Affordable Healthcare Act in 2010, it included section 4205, the menu labeling provision. This was the first time there would be a national law requiring restaurants or similar retail food establishments with 20 or more locations to provide calorie and nutrition information to consumers. The purpose was to address the issue of obesity in our country and give people a way to make more informed decisions about the food they eat outside of their homes. Some smaller parts of the country already had local or even state laws in place requiring menu labeling, but this was set to be Federal Mandated National implementation.

It was a law, but I knew there would be discussion with the FDA before it became mandatory. I assumed it would take maybe a couple of years, and it would probably be in place by 2012, or worst case, 2013. MenuTrinfo® gave restaurants an effective way to get nutrition information and calorie counts out to their clients through our newly formed restaurant nutritional help desk service and our software. Back in 2010, there were some big chain restaurants already doing this mostly for themselves, but once the law was enacted, I knew we would be slammed with business.

In the meantime, I didn't want to wait around for the government to put everything in place. What I thought would be a year or two has turned into more than eight plus. It was time to pivot, to create a branch of the company that could bring in income and sustain us while we waited.

MenuTrinfo® provided a way for businesses to get nutrition information to pass on to their consumers and help those with allergies, food sensitivities, and celiac disease make informed decisions when eating out. When giving a talk at the Maryland Restaurant show in 2010 on menu labeling and food allergies and how it impacts restaurants today, I came away with the second part of the business already forming in my head. Why not expand on this and create a training program for those in the foodservice industry to help them better accommodate those clients? That's when AllerTrain™ was born.

AllerTrain™® is an ANSI (American National Standards Institute) accredited food allergy and gluten-free training course, the very first one of its kind. It teaches food service professionals about the top foods causing food allergies, the proper protocol for preparing food to avoid cross-contact, and how to better serve diners with special dietary needs. This helps restaurants avoid allergy related incidents and prepares them to handle such incidents, should they occur.

It has taken many years to build AllerTrain™ to the level it is today, but we started teaching the classes in 2011 with a few huge restaurant brands, and that started the income headed our way. After the success of the basic AllerTrain™ class, we realized we needed more than a one-size-fits-all training program, so we created specific variations. We now have 11 different training courses, including ones tailored for universities, school districts, manufacturers, and pizzerias with additional food safety training to be launched in the very near future. The sky truly is the limit for where we can go with this line of service offerings in the business.

To succeed in business, you have to be ready to pivot—to adjust and make changes to keep your company relevant and be the leader in your industry. If I had put all my eggs in one basket and relied solely on menu labeling services as my source of revenue, I'd be struggling or most likely gone like so many others. As I write this, menu labeling still has not been enacted and mandatory for restaurants to comply. It continues to get pushed back with the latest date of compliance now May 7, 2018. But, because of my persistence and willingness to adjust, I have a sustainable, now million-dollar business. As of today, both sides of the company generate income, but there will probably come a day when one side or the other takes the lead.

If I were to guess, I would say in the long run, allergy training will make more than nutrition, but then again, we recently pivoted and launched an additional line of business with kitchen audits and certification. Maybe that horse will lead, who knows? Because we were willing to pivot and go for it, we are not a one-product company. This variety allows us allows us to stay in business and grow stronger as a result.

It Doesn't Hurt to Ask and Ask and Ask...

Back in the early days of my business, I was helping with a state restaurant trade show in the southeastern part of the country. My job was to find a speaker to talk about food allergies. With tasks like this, I always reach for the top. Why not learn from the best? I contacted a gentleman associated with a large theme park who had an incredible amount of experience serving those with food allergies.

I tracked down his name, then his phone number, and called his office. A woman answered the phone.

"My name is Betsy Craig," I told her. "I am looking to put a panel together at the state trade show on serving those with food allergies. May I speak with Chef?"

"Of course," she said. "One moment, please."

She put me through to him, and I explained who I was and why I was calling. "I'd be honored if you could come speak at the conference to share your knowledge and expertise with everyone there. Your locations have been the gold standard in the industry at addressing the needs of hundreds of thousands of customers with food allergies each year. Those attending the event could learn so much from you. Are you interested and willing to join me on this panel?"

"Thanks for contacting me. It sounds like a great opportunity," he said. "But, I need to get permission to do something like this. I will see what I can do and get back to you."

"No problem. I understand," I said. "I will call you back in a week or so to see how it is looking." Before I let him off the phone, I got his direct extension, so I could go right to his desk on the next phone call to him.

I waited two weeks and nothing. I called back and left Chef a message. No response. I called back four more times and left messages. My guess is his lack of a response was because he was busy, didn't have an answer from his higher ups yet, or he hoped I would go away. Not going to happen with me, as he learned.

Finally, he answered a call.

"Hey, Betsy. Nice to hear from you, and thanks for your patience," he said. "I got your messages. It would be my pleasure to speak to the group."

"Thank you! This is great," I said. "I have one more favor. The day before the trade show begins, there is going to be a gluten-free pizza contest. I am a judge for that, but we need one more person. Would you like to join me?"

"Sure," he said. "I'd be happy to."

I ask, and ask for more, and when I am done with that, I might even ask for one final thing. Why not? The worst anyone has ever said to me is no, and believe me, no's do not stop me in business or in life.

While we sat there at the conference a few months later, eating and judging pizza, he asked about me and my company. I told him all about MenuTrinfo® and the allergy training we do. I explained our software and how it can identify allergens in food. He asked lots of questions and shared with me that his company has software they utilized in order to pull up the numbers they needed. It was a great conversation, and to be honest, I never dreamed it could ever go anywhere.

With the business-related questions out of the way, the conversation turned to the usual, getting-to-know each other questions. Turns out we grew up in the same part of upstate New York in two adjacent small towns. We had great time talking about the area and shared stories with each other.

The gluten-free pizza contest was a success, and when he gave his presentation, the room overflowed with people standing three-deep everywhere you looked. Everyone loved hearing him. Years later, he told me he had started out hoping I would give up and stop calling. But once we did connect, he said it was my passion and persistence that won him over.

After the trade show, Chef and I went our separate ways, back to our own companies. Months later, on a Monday afternoon, he called out of the blue.

"Hey, Betsy, it's Chef. Can I hire your company to run some numbers for me? It is for a few menu items. I am really curious to know where your software would put these numbers."

"Of course," I said. "I am happy to help. When do you need the information?"

"It's going to be tight, but I need it in three days, and we'd like to have a conference call to discuss the findings on Friday," he said. "Is this something your company can do?"

"Absolutely!" I said, not really knowing how I was going to pull this off. I always say yes then figure out how to accomplish that yes. This was no exception. The size of potential client or work load doesn't matter. We are a company that begins with yes.

I got the information I needed from him, set the time for the meeting at the end of that week, and got to work entering the recipes into our system in order to get the reports he needed. This was a huge deal. If I could help a reputable, well-known company of this size, it could be great for my business. I planned to do whatever it took to make this happen and show them we were top caliber when it came to menu labeling. They did not need to know I worked in my basement and only had two part-time employees.

The conference call was scheduled for Friday. I needed to make a good impression, so I invited a friend, who was a registered dietician, to be there as a consultant to answer any questions about nutrition. Rocky knew he could handle hundreds of thousands of recipes from these folks, and he was there to answer software questions. I planned to lead the call on our end and talk about our company.

My biggest apprehension about the meeting was our dog. I didn't want Chef and his people to know MenuTrinfo® was headquartered in my basement at that time. I wanted them to feel confident that we were a big enough company to handle their business and show our professionalism. That might not happen if the dog started barking in the middle of the call.

Friday arrived. With Rocky and my friend down in the basement in the "office," it was time for operation "Keep the Dog Quiet." It was a nice day, so I put the her outside and taped up her dog door so she couldn't get in. I closed the back door and stuck a towel along the opening on the bottom to keep any sound from seeping in. Then I closed the basement door and prayed that my safeguards would do the trick.

The three of us sat around the table with the phone in the middle. My heart raced, and I wondered if the dog would find another way to sneak into the house. When we were ready, I made the call.

Rocky explained how he created the software by taking the USDA Database of information and pulling it into a database he built which added other variables and equations, including absorptions, marinades, frying and cooking methods, and tagging allergens. He took as much human factor and error out as he possibly could. He built it to accommodate hundreds of thousands of recipes, and this gigantic database is hidden behind two firewalls, backed up to another server, and every week it goes to a vault.

I then explained how the program takes into account cooking times, temperatures, and how the food is prepared in order to get accurate numbers. To this day, I still don't know how many people were in the conference room on their end, nor do I really care. We just told our truth, shared what we learned, and how our numbers came to be.

Over the course of the conversation, we heard their people in the background say, "Ours doesn't do that."

I explained it also figures in oil absorption, steaming, and marinating.

We heard again, "Ours doesn't do that."

By the time we wrapped up the call, we had answered all their questions, and they seemed pleased with our answers and the numbers we provided them for their eight recipes.

Nine months later, I got a call back from Chef saying they needed us to help them again, but this time it was a few more recipes. They signed on as a client, and this was a company making deal for me; it was huge. It meant a lot that this company trusted us with their nutritional numbers, and now I could afford to rent an office. It felt like a major step forward. The best way I can describe it is there was my business life before this client, which took place in my basement, and then life after this client came on. We moved into an office space overlooking downtown where I don't have to worry about the dog barking. They stayed with us for three+ years with our monthly program, and now they call us when they need us.

None of this would have happened if I had given up on trying to get Chef to come speak at that restaurant show. I persisted, and in the long run, it landed me a friend, and my company an amazing client.

Head to Head with FDA

Saying this with a little smile in my voice, I tormented the FDA (Food and Drug Administration). I did it on behalf of my good friends in the pizza industry because changes needed to happen with nutrition labeling of pizza, and I planned to do everything in my power to see that they did.

The FDA came out and said pizzerias had to calculate the calories either by the slice or by the whole pizza pie. Those were the only two options they could put on their menus. An immediate problem surfaced because there was something called Chicago party cut, or even in other parts of the country, St Louis cut, where a round pizza is cut into squares or different shapes. This affected a very good friend of mine and client, president of a 200+ pizza concept out of Chicago. She was very vocal in our industry, expressing her concern about the mandate as it placed her company at an unfair disadvantage compared to other pizza concepts just because of the way they sliced their pizza. In one article, she was quoted as saying, "It will be extremely difficult to compete with Dominos or Pizza Hut next door that can list their pizza at 300 calories per slice instead of a whole pizza that might have 3,000 calories."

I wanted to help my buddy and our other clients who wanted to provide accurate information to their consumers. It was time to call the FDA.

I explained the problem to the woman on the phone.

She responded, "Because none of the slices are the same size with this kind of cut, pizzerias have to put the calorie count for the full pizza."

I said, "You are truly harming those clients of ours that do party cut."

She said, "We're sorry, but that's the way it is."

"We'll see about that," I said.

I called back a couple weeks later, and the same scenario played out. But this time, I suggested they adopt the same standard they already have for grocery store pizzas which is by the ounce and not by the size. This makes it more accurate because it is not being affected by who cuts the pizza.

The response, "Sorry, but restaurants have to abide by the current regulations and use calorie counts based on a triangle slice or the full pizza."

I refused to give up. I kept calling and calling. For a year (2015), at every single event the FDA hosted for our industry explaining menu labeling, we had someone attend and beat on this question. My company emailed this question as well and wasn't ready to accept the answer they provided. I wanted to make them understand they were not doing what was right for a whole sector of the pizza business. It took over two years, but because of my efforts, being unstoppable to the FDA, and those of others in the industry, we convinced them the changes were necessary. We can now do the menu labeling per piece, even on party cut, and have saved the emails to back that up. What I know today is that technically what I did was called lobbying. Who knew? Whatever it is called, it takes persistence and hutzpah to get laws and regulations changed, but when I believe in something to my core, I won't back down. I may change angles or methods to be heard, but I always keep going and keep fighting until the door slams in my face, or I get what I am fighting for.

When the Rug Gets Pulled Out

Seven years after the Affordable Health Care Act was signed, menu labeling as a law for chain restaurants with over 20 locations was supposed to go into effect, Friday, May 5, 2017. Many big restaurants already provided their consumers with nutrition information, but this would make it a requirement. Delays had happened over the years, and in April, I heard rumors it might get postponed again. This time, I had high hopes it would go through, and I ran my business as if the new law would start on this date. My employees had been putting in tons of extra hours to get all the numbers in place for our clients before the deadline.

May came and everything seemed on track. After all these years, menu labeling was finally going to be made into law, or so I thought.

Two big lobbying groups in D.C. pushed back. They wrote a letter on the first of May to the White House, saying they wanted one more year to implement menu labeling. On May 4, one day before the new laws were going to be put into effect, the FDA delayed again due to their own recommendation on their own law. This is so crazy even I could not make this stuff up!

My whole company had worked overtime as we moved toward this deadline. We had lots of clients counting on us getting them the information so that they would be ready for May 5th. Now, the urgency disappeared overnight, and the future of MenuTrinfo® was left hanging in the balance.

When I walked into the work that Tuesday morning, May 2nd, after the news broke there would be yet another delay, the air felt like it had been sucked out of the office. A heavy weight filled the space. We were all stunned, and my employees feared they may lose their jobs.

I called my entire staff together.

"I know that this is not the outcome we wanted or anticipated. We can't change it. We just have to deal with it the best we can. I understand some of you may be worried about the company and your job, but I need you to hang in there. I'm going out of town for a few days to clear my head and figure out a plan. I need you all to run the office while I am gone."

The time away allowed me to process all that had happened. I gave myself permission to be angry for a little bit but then moved on just like when I was sick. Be mad, get done being mad, and then get into action. I got quiet, I prayed, I ran through different scenarios until I had a plan. It was time to pivot again!

I called all my nutrition staff together. They were the ones most concerned about their jobs since it was the nutritional help desk that went from manic calls, emails, and needs to silence overnight.

"You can all stop worrying. You will still have full-time jobs, and your salaries will remain the same. However, your responsibilities are going to shift."

You could feel the collective sigh of relief in the room as I continued, "We currently have 60+ nutrition clients, so each of you will do menu labeling for ¼ to ½ of your day. The rest of your time will be spent on other tasks. One of you will move over to AllerTrain™ full time where we need more help."

I walked over to another nutrition team member and said, "Since our administrative assistant was not retained past his probation period last week, I am moving you to this position."

I felt the tension in the room dissipate, heads began to nod positively, knowing it was going to be ok.

"I am grateful for each and every one of you, and together we will get through this. You all rock!"

Persistence in the professional world is more than just not giving up. It is about staying the course and being true to yourself and your business. It's about fighting for who and what you believe in. My focus over the years has changed. It is now less about how many pairs of shoes I have and more about making sure others have shoes. Of course, I want my company to be profitable, in fact, finally hitting that million mark has been a strong goal for a very long time. But my core mission stems from being that voice for those with food allergies, making sure they have safe options when they dine out, protecting lives and health through nutrition and training. That's what we do, daily. The people come first, and the money, which it is necessary to keep things going, is second.

My passion, combined with my persistence, makes me a force to be reckoned with. I am not going to stop believing something is possible until the door is fully closed and locked. I will continue to have hope and keep trying until that happens. It makes some around me a little crazy that I don't back down. But I tell them, I was raised by an angry German, so I know how to hold my position and stick to my mission.

Persistence: Food for Thought

➢ Take a moment to reflect on your attitude and views toward money. Do you feel it is a healthy view, or are there areas you feel you need to work on? If so, what are those areas, and what steps will you take to improve your attitudes?

➢ Think back to a time in your career or business when you gave up too soon. What did you learn from that? What will you do differently next time?

➢ Reflect on a time with your business or career when your drive and persistence pushed you to accomplish an amazing task. How did it make you feel?

➢ Think back to a time with work or at home when you had to pivot and change your direction. How did it work out? If you could do it all again, would you do handle it the same way? If not, what would you do differently?

CHAPTER 7

Courage Is Fear That Has Said Its Prayers

Spiritual Principle: Courage

cour·age (noun) the ability to do something that frightens one.

In 1985, I learned a great acronym for FEAR, False Evidence Appearing Real, and it still resonates with me today. We build up doubts, insecurities, and anxiety to the point where we give fear the power to hold us hostage. Sometimes it is for justified reasons, like a car accident, loss of a job, or an illness, and other times, it can be simple analysis paralysis, looking at life with fear glasses and expecting nothing to work out the right way. It can keep us from fulfilling our life's purpose, sharing our gifts and talents with others, or experiencing personal growth.

Courage is the ability to face those fears and walk right through them. It is something we have complete control over. Whether in life or in business, the ability to stand up for yourself and take risks involves courage. Many times, it actually doesn't feel like a choice, that's one of the tricky things with FEAR.

When I think of FEAR, I remember a little saying from my past that goes like this:

FEAR knocked on the door

FAITH answered

NO ONE was there

Walking Through the Fear

In my late teens, it didn't matter what the question was, alcohol was always my answer.

When I was lucky enough to get sober, I had to give up my best friend, my solution—alcohol—and face life without a buffer. I woke up each day wondering *how in God's name am I going to make it through today?* Doing normal tasks completely sober made me break out in a cold sweat. Whether it was going to the grocery store or going out on a sales call, it didn't matter, facing it sober terrified me. I had to dig deep inside myself, phone a friend for help, or go to prayer each time to find any morsel of courage to get through these situations.

During the first six months of my sobriety, my life started to slip away. All my horrible decisions and actions while I had been wasted came back to haunt me. I had not lived up to a good deal of my obligations, and now, I had to face them all and do it stone cold sober. My furniture was repossessed. I was evicted, and I owed over $20,000 in medical bills (thanks to not making medical insurance a priority over my addictions). It felt like a horrible domino effect with each day tipping over another tile.

I had just turned 21. After getting kicked out of the room I was renting in my friends' condo, I turned to my parents for help. Considering everything I went through growing up, I never thought I would end up back with them, but I had no other options. Low doesn't even come close to describe how I felt having to move into their basement. But getting sober and getting my emotional and spiritual life on track kept me looking toward the future despite this rough patch.

Through early sobriety, I had managed to maintain a job as an on-the-road sales rep selling paper goods, small wares, table top and other non-food items to restaurants and hotels. I spent a lot of time in my car—the one thing that hadn't been taken away yet.

The oil light kept coming on, and it bugged me. I covered it up with tape, so I didn't have to look at it. By turning up the radio, the clicking noise coming from the engine couldn't be heard. I had no idea that if a car didn't have oil, it would break down. I learned the hard way when the clicking became banging, then a really loud noise, and then the car stopped working. That was followed by lots of smoke from the engine and a stream of obscenities from me. Tears ran down my cheeks. I wondered how people lived without Jack Daniels because at that moment, it was the only thing I wanted. Terrified of what to do next, I reached for a phone to call a friend instead of a bottle. It was a simple thing to do but a gigantic turning point for me.

I had no money for a car and zero credit, so I knew getting another one wasn't an option. Creditors kept calling me about my debts, and the bank didn't appreciate all my bounced checks. My money managing skills were non-existent, as I had never learned how to handle finances responsibly. Now, without a car, I had no way to do my job. For almost 2 weeks, I led my boss to believe I was still working by calling my clients and getting their orders over the phone, calling them in as if I had visited the account, and hoping he would not recognize things were amiss.

The following Monday morning, I woke up in a cold sweat. I called in sick to work that day, but I expect they knew I was not physically sick. Looking back, I think I was spiritually sick and felt my life had no direction. My job was in jeopardy, and I didn't know what to do. Fear began to consume my thoughts. Since I was committed to not drinking, I once again reached for the phone. I took a deep breath and called a good friend who I am still in contact with to this day.

He answered, "What do you need, honey?"

"I need a ride to visit with some friends," I said.

"Where are you?" he asked.

"I am under my bed," I answered, not even realizing how crazy that must have sounded.

"I see. I will come get you," he said, "But you're going to have to be brave. When I beep the horn, I will be in your driveway, and it will be safe to come out."

"Ok," I said, and I hung up. My heart raced as I listened for the car and fought off the darkness that tried to consume me.

Minutes dragged on until finally, I heard the horn. I climbed out from under the bed and ran to the car. We went to meet up with our friends for a while, and afterward, I felt a little better.

An older guy named Ed (may he rest in peace), came over to me and said, "Let's go to lunch."

"I don't have any money," I said.

"I didn't ask you if you had any damn money, I said 'let's go to lunch.'" He grinned.

"Alright. Will you drop me home after?" I asked.

"Yes."

"Why do you look so sad?" Ed asked at the restaurant.

"Well, I owe a lot of money; I barely have enough to survive. I have to go to court for bounced checks. I'm living in my parent's basement, and that's not the place I want to be. My car is dead. I just turned 21. My job's in jeopardy, and I don't know what the hell to do next." I took a breath holding back the tears.

He looked at me and said, "Are you going to suck your thumb in your parent's basement the rest of your life, or are you going to do something about it?"

I stared at him, shocked. I needed help, or support, or encouragement, and instead, I had this old scruffy guy sitting in front of me being mean to me.

"I-I don't know what to do," I whispered.

"This is what you are going to do," he said. "Did you pray today? Did you turn your life over to anything today?"

"Well, no," I said.

"Well, it's about time you did. Why don't you turn it over and get into action?"

"But I have 18 creditors after me, and I can't pay them."

"You need to ask God to step in. Then, you need to call every one of those creditors and tell them you can pay $5/month, $10/month, $2/month... They just need to hear from you, honey. They don't care what the number is."

"Really?" I asked.

"Yes, really," he said, "Then, I want you to call your boss and tell him you are working on getting a car. It won't be a surprise to him you are without one. You will give him an honest answer within 24 hours about what type of transportation you have. You get that he knows you haven't been doing your job, right? And you need to do your job."

"Right," I said. "This sucks, Ed. But I'll do it."

"Honey, no one said it's going to be easy. Doing the right thing, facing these fears, is not easy but will feel so much better on the back side, I promise you. Time to face them head on today."

He dropped me off at home and every part of me wanted to crawl back under that bed and pretend none of this was happening. To say I was terrified was an understatement. But if Ed thought this was going to work, then I would trust him.

I sat on my bed and said, "Ok, God, whoever you are, if you are up there, I need you to step in because I need your help."

For the next few hours, I called all 18 creditors. I told a Hospital in Maryland that I could give them $10 a month towards the $2,380.00 I owed them, and the women on the phone said, "That's more than we are getting from you now."

After making all those calls, relief washed over me. I could answer the phone again. I could open the mail again. Fear had caused me to ignore my responsibilities. As I stood there enjoying this moment, I heard a knock at my door.

I opened it, and this acquaintance of mine I met through friends like Ed, stood there smiling at me.

"Hey, Bets," he said, "Ed told me you need a car."

"I do," I said, a little confused and unsure about what was going on.

"Ed told me you don't have any credit," he said.

"No, Chris, I don't have any credit. I have to go to court because I have bounced checks. I actually have less than no credit." The words spilled out of my mouth as I felt relief in sharing the burden of the challenges I saw no end to.

He laughed, "Come on. Get in my car, let's go for a ride."

"Where are we going?" I asked.

"I'm going to get you a car."

I hesitated, thinking *what do I have to do to pay for this?* And then I thought, *I've done worse.* He was a sweet guy, but sober everything does look a little different. I got in the car, and we went to a used car lot. He told me to pick the car I wanted. I picked this huge black car that can best be described as a pimp mobile.

"This one will work," I said.

He paused, "Are you sure?"

"Yes, I can drive it, and it's only a couple thousand dollars."

We went into the dealer to the financing department. The guy behind the desk asked for my social security number.

"Chris, this is not going to work," I said.

"Just give him your number," he said.

I did as he asked. Then the guy turned to Chris who gave the man his social security number.

"How long do you want the finance the car for?" the guy asked.

I looked at Chris, "You don't have to do this."

"I know," he said.

He looked at the finance guy and told him I could only afford $100 per month. "Does that work?" he asked me.

"Yes," I nodded.

The papers were drawn, Chris signed on the bottom line, and now I had a car.

We were getting ready to leave the lot in our separate cars, and I said to Chris, "How can I pay you for this? What can I do for you?"

"Make your payments on time, stay sober, and pass it on." He smiled, got in his car, and left.

I watched him drive off, and I knew I would do everything in my power to hold up my end of the deal, and I did. I never missed a payment, was always on time, and try to this day to always pay it forward whenever possible.

During this time in my life, I needed courage to get me through everyday tasks. Basic responsibilities that were second nature to most people weighed heavy on me and caused great anxiety. But fear, actual or perceived, still feels scary. Whether it is in life or business, we must face it head on and walk through it. We can't let fear contain us and keep us from achieving success.

Hit Me with Whatever Just Save My Fingers!

With my Scleroderma, I have faced fear head on more times than I'd like. Each time I do what Ed told me all those years ago, and I turn it over to God. Then I dig deep inside to pull together all the courage I can. Then I suit up, show up, grow up, and stand up to the fear and move past it.

When my fingers were rotting, I told the doctor he could try anything he thought would help, if it could possibly save my fingers and my life. I knew the results I wanted, but I had no context to truly understand how big this figurative treatment was going to be.

The doctor planned to give me prostacyclin, an insanely strong drug, to open up the blood vessels. The procedure needed to be done in ICU because when all your blood vessels are opened up, there is a high chance of bleeding out. They wanted a nurse within arms-length of me the whole time.

They explained everything to me, and I was on board, terrified, but on board. I felt pretty good about it all and confident it would all work out. The day before being admitted to the hospital, I got a call from the hospital pharmacy.

"Is this Betsy?" said the pharmacist. "Are you aware of what you're about to do?"

"Yes," I said. "My doctor explained it to me."

"Did you know we have never administered this drug at this hospital before?" she said.

"Um, no, I didn't." My heart, my stomach, my nerves all realized the severity of the situation at the same time.

"This is a powerful drug," she said. "You just need to know what you are setting yourself up for and what the precautions are for it. I want to make sure you are well informed."

"I understand," I told her. "Thanks for calling." I took a few deep breaths. I knew I needed this procedure, but I also knew I needed every ounce of courage to walk into the hospital the next day.

With Rocky by my side, I faced the fear and went to the ICU the next day to check in. It didn't help that the doctors and nurses all seemed nervous and scared about the procedure. One nurse came into the room carrying the syringe in a bag with two hands like she was carrying a precious newborn preemie. She gently set it down. If it was dropped, it seemed the drug would do something like explode and no longer be valid. I had never seen anyone carry a medication like that before (or since) in my life.

Between the medical staff being on edge and knowing this potent poison was about to be pumped through my system, I had to have faith. I had to have courage and believe it would work. My favorite prayer came to mind, and I just started reciting it, "God grant me the serenity to accept the things I cannot change, the courage to change the things I can, and the wisdom to know the difference," over and over for what felt like a hundred times.

I spent five days in the hospital. They would pump the drug into me for eight hours, then I'd sit for 16 hours and play backgammon with my husband. Then they would pump it into me for another eight hours, then I'd sit for the next 16. Every hour, they tested my vitals to make sure I was not having an adverse reaction from the meds. This continued over and over for 120 hours.

The drug was miserable and harsh. I couldn't swallow, and it felt like a thousand nerve endings throughout my body were all exposed. At one point, the nurse that sat next to my bed dropped her pen, and it rolled across the floor. She called somebody to come and pick it up. She wouldn't leave my side even to walk across the room to get the pen.

After enduring the treatment for almost a week, I was glad when it was done. Overall it was success; it did open the blood vessels throughout my body. The problem was, following some testing, the doctor concluded that clots had formed at the end of my rotting fingers. The blood was still not getting to my fingertips.

A week later he called, "I haven't given up on healing your fingers. I'd like to try something else."

If it meant getting past this, I was willing to be a guinea pig. "Yeah," I said, "Let's try it!"

"I'm going to push nitroglycerin down there to see if we can break up the clots and open up those veins," he said. "Hopefully, that will get some blood back into your fingers."

"Will it hurt?" I asked.

"No, not really," he said. "You will feel it, but it will be a crazy and unusual sensation."

The treatment was bizarre. It was like downing a milk jug full of espresso, except this was ten times stronger. My heart raced, and I was jittery. It was a huge rush that last about two minutes but felt like hours.

The final result? Within a week, I felt a warm sensation at the ends of my fingers; something I hadn't felt for months. I was ecstatic and so grateful. This didn't make the scleroderma go away (nothing could do that), but it did solve the issues with my fingers.

Both of these procedures scared me almost to death, and there are times when a little fear is a good thing. These were potentially dangerous measures, and it made sense to be apprehensive. The problem comes when we let the fear immobilize us. It will keep us frozen and not allow us to grow or move past something. If I had let my emotions and worries consume me regarding these procedures, I would not have my fingers today. Challenges will always be a part of life, and there are times when we must dig up the courage to face them head on in order to open up our life for new possibilities.

Courage in the Small Things

Sometimes even small tasks or requests can cause anxiety. It can feel easier to turn back around rather than being brave and walking through the fear and uncomfortable feelings.

At one point with my disease, I traveled back and forth to Denver a lot for doctor's appointments. Out of 20 work days one month, I had 16 different doctor appointments. I was tired, my husband was tired, and my daughter was tired of not seeing her mom.

On one occasion, I was scheduled to see two different doctors for some testing: one a lung doc and one a GI doc. The night before, I hit a wall where I knew I couldn't physically do the 90-minute drive there. Rocky was exhausted. I needed to find someone willing to take me.

I was talking to my mentor who lived in California. She said, "You need to text everyone in your network to see who is free tomorrow, and who can take you."

"Nobody will do that for me," I told her. "It's a last-minute request. It's 8:00 PM now, and I have to leave tomorrow morning at 7:00 AM. Plus, it's an all-day thing."

"I don't know if anyone can help, but I do know you need to ask," she said.

"Alright, I'll do it," I said.

Even though I told her that, I really didn't want to. I didn't want to be a burden on anyone and fear filled my head with thoughts of *what if nobody can help or nobody wants to help.* Desperation kicked in, and I ignored the voice in my head.

I put out a group text:

I have to go to Denver tomorrow, and my mentor doesn't want me driving because I am worn out. I hate to bug everyone, but is there anyone who can drive me to Denver tomorrow for two doctors' appointments that will take all day?

A woman answered right away. "What time do you want me at your door and do you want a Starbucks?"

I'll be darned; she showed up that next day, drove me to Denver, sat through all my different appointments, then drove me home, all with sweetness in her voice and kindness in her heart.

At the end of the day, she couldn't stop thanking me for including her in part of my journey. I was touched by her thoughtfulness and willingness to give up her day to help me. Had I let fear stop me, I am not sure what I would have done, and I would have taken away this opportunity for her to be of service to me which she seemed truly grateful for. This experience made our friendship strong, and I will do just about anything for her and her for me.

Don't Back Down When You Know You Are Right

It was October 2010, and I had only been in business eight months. Over these initial months, I spoke at various small events regarding menu labeling and food allergies. Now I was on my way to speak at the annual Fast Casual Restaurant event in Chicago.

This exclusive event is reserved for top-level restaurant executives who are leaders in the fast-casual industry. This would be the first time I'd be talking to CEOs, Presidents, and COOs of major restaurant chains. I enjoy talking to people, and felt confident in my knowledge of the topic, but this one made me a little nervous. With my company being new, I was still in the process of networking and connecting with others in the industry, so I didn't know the major players yet.

I checked into the Sofitel in Chicago, an elaborate and gorgeous hotel. I kept thinking *how the hell did I end up here?* The topic for my ½ of an hour-long session was the impact the new Affordable Health Care Act would have on the restaurant industry. I was to talk about menu labeling, and another gentleman planned to talk about health insurance.

It was scheduled as the last session of the day, and unlike the others throughout the day that had been broken into two tracks, all 400+ attendees would be at this presentation. It was my chance to establish myself as the leading subject matter expert on the topic. Tons of pressure, more fear.

People filed into the room, talking and laughing as they found their way to seats at one of the many round tables set up in the room. The food industry is a very close-knit community where everyone is super friendly and positive. There had been a lot of good sessions that day, and those were being discussed.

Then it came time for our session. A heavy blanket seemed to drop over the crowd and silence filled the room. The seriousness of what Obamacare was going to do to the restaurant business took over. People were concerned about the impact health care benefits and menu labeling was going to have on their companies.

The speaker talking about benefits went first and left the crowd with more questions than answers. I wanted to leave them with more answers than questions. I did my presentation, and then we opened it up for Q&A.

Directly in front of me sat a gentleman, his business partner, and his entourage. As soon as I asked if there were any question, he jumped right in. He was definitely a dominant force in the room.

It was clear from the beginning, he had a sour attitude about the government stepping in and requiring more mandates for the restaurant industry. He felt it was a burden, and he was not the Lone Ranger with that opinion in the room.

He fired off his questions to me.

"Who is going to police the menu labeling?"

"How do you intend to be accurate with your information when the USDA database is outdated?"

"How can you handle variances in meat and cooking?"

With every question, I stood my ground and answered his questions. I felt the tension in the room rise, but I maintained my poise and felt confident in the information I gave him. You could hear a pin drop through the entire exchange.

He fired one last question.

"How can you guarantee the accuracy of the information your company provides? I think this is ridiculous that they want us to guarantee it when nobody can do that."

I took a deep breath, stood a little taller, and responded.

"Look, I can tell you're mad, but I didn't cause it. This is what we have to work with. My company will work, to the best of our ability, to insure our information is correct. In fact, we guarantee our work and accuracy. Menu labeling has been on packages in the grocery store for 20 years; it is time for it to be on our take-out containers."

He looked at me and smiled.

"Young lady, I owe you a case of wine (which is so funny for me). You gave me great answers, and you don't back down."

"No, sir, I don't."

Silence filled the room. There were no more questions, so we thanked everyone, and the session was over. People came up after, including this gentleman, who shook my hand and said, "You did a fine job presenting. Thank you."

My new best friend waited and then came up to me after he left. "Do you know who you just argued with in front of hundreds of executives?"

"I have no idea," I said.

She grinned, told me who he was, and said, "He's huge in the business world, and you held your own against him. Great job."

"Really?" I said. "Good to know."

The icing on the cake was I ended up sitting with him and his crew at dinner that night and heard precious stories of the industry dating back 30+ years. It was fascinating, educational, and at the end of the night, my face hurt from smiling and having a blast.

Courage can be defined as the attitude of facing and dealing with anything recognized as dangerous, difficult, or painful, instead of withdrawing from it. Standing on that stage in front of all those executives wasn't dangerous or painful, but it wasn't easy. Especially while being grilled with questions meant to shake me up. It was courage and my unwavering knowledge of my subject matter that gave me the confidence to not back down when confronted.

During my presentation, I made an impression, not only on with my new friend, but on everyone else in that room. I got a call three weeks ago from a gentleman who was there during this talk, and now he wants to hire my company, seven years later. He remembered me being self-assured, confident, and detailed when I talked about menu-labeling. Never under estimate the power of a first impression.

He said, "Here are my two brands and what we have done so far. I don't trust our numbers, we need your help."

"Of course, we can help you," I said.

Having the courage to face challenging situations head on, or to push yourself up against your comfort zones, will allow for growth in your business. Others in your industry will see your strength and confidence and look to you as leader in your field.

Courage: Food for Thought

➢ Reflect on a time in your personal life when you faced a fear and walked through it. Now reflect on a time with your business or career. With each of these experiences, how did you feel when it was all over?

➢ Do these fears still have a hold on you today? If so, what actions can you take to minimize those?

➢ What is an area in your life where you wish you'd had more courage?

➢ How would your life be different if you faced that fear?

➢ What are three actions you can take to make that happen?

Every day, we come across tasks, people, or situations that stir up fear for us. It could be you are avoiding a conversation with someone, putting off finishing an assignment for fear it isn't going to be good enough, or maybe there is something you need to let go of. Reflect on that, and then write down as many as you can think of. Over the next 30 days, make it a point to face one of those each day and walk through that fear.

CHAPTER 8

Education Comes in Many Ways

Spiritual Principle: Wisdom

wis·dom (noun) the body of knowledge and principles that develops within a specified society or period.

E ducation and as a result, wisdom, comes in all shapes and sizes and can be so much more than just earning a degree. Don't get me wrong, I believe college is important, and it is a belief I instilled in my daughter as she was growing up. But, studying at a university isn't the only way to gain the knowledge and wisdom needed to be the CEO of a successful company.

When I became sober and started applying spiritual principles to my life, it was clear to me that I had to learn a lot of things by the seat of my pants. Instead of attending the University of Colorado, I attended the University of Life, which I refer to as the school of hard knocks. It was a hard set of courses, and instead of grades, it was strictly pass/fail.

Along the way, I met amazing mentors and teachers who imparted their wisdom to me. They taught me lessons that helped me be a better business owner by sharing their insights and experiences which can't be learned from books. These ideas and wisdom all became ingredients in my recipe for success in my life today.

The World Owes You Nothing

At 22 years old, I was two years into sobriety and living with these new spiritual principles. Even though I was very busy, I decided I wanted to go back to school. Tired of working, I felt someone should pay my way. Most young adults get their parents to pay for college. My mom and dad believed in education at the principle of it all, but I knew better. They weren't going to pay for squat.

At that time, I lived with my boyfriend. I told him he should work while I went to school. I didn't even ask. I just approached it from an entitlement mindset that told me I deserved this. It was what I refer to as my "Princess Phase" because I felt the world owed me something since I had a crappy childhood. This worked for a few months, then real life stepped in. I went from really entitled to really broke really fast. My boyfriend had a job and earned money, but it wasn't enough to pay all the bills. The lesson came flying at me at full speed. It doesn't matter how much sweet talking you do, if you want to live in a house, you better pay your rent.

Not wanting to move, I quit school and went back to being a waitress. I knew how to throw a tray above my head and sling drinks. This time though, I was stone cold sober, splashing gin and tonics on myself instead of down my throat. Each night I came home with $150-$200, and it allowed us to pay the bills and stay in the house.

After a while, I realized no one owed me anything. People were not lining up at my door saying, "Poor Betsy. You had a horrible childhood. Here's some money to make up for that." They had their own lives to deal with without worrying about me. It became clear, if I wanted something, I needed to make it happen. Since I wasn't a real princess, this was real life 101. If I wanted to go to school, so be it, but I had to figure out how to pay the rent first.

This lesson has helped me throughout my adult life, especially with my business. Becoming a successful CEO of a company didn't happen by having the attitude that the world owed me something. That's not how it works. It didn't matter that I was out on my own at 17, or that I was raising a teenage daughter, or that I had a disease that wanted me dead. Waiting for a hand-out or for someone to feel sorry for me wasn't going to get me anywhere. Becoming successful takes hard work, determination, and perseverance to produce the desired results. Period.

Suit Up, Show Up, and Grow Up

Early on when I was trying to stay sober, I had a mentor in my life, Dawn. She told me to call her every single day to let her know how I was doing. And she meant it. Within a month, although not on purpose, I skipped two days in a row of calling her because I felt like she really didn't mean it, and I didn't want to bug her.

On the third day, I finally called her.

"Hi, Dawn," I said. "It's Betsy, I am calling to check in."

"Honey, are you ok?" she said. "You haven't called me in two days. What's going on?"

Stunned she cared, I answered, "I'm sorry I didn't call you."

"Why didn't you call?"

"I hate to keep bugging you," I said.

"How dare you deny me the right to help you?" she said. "I told you to call me every day. Do you have problems following directions?"

"No, ma'am." (The funny thing is I don't remember ever calling someone ma'am before. Respect started for me at that moment.)

"Because when I said every day, I meant every single day. Every day ending in Y, you call me."

"Yes, ma'am. I understand."

I never missed another phone call. I called from vacation, from the hospital, from anywhere and everywhere, but I never missed two days in a row again in the many years that followed. Dawn taught me to respect myself and others, and if I say I am going to do something or be somewhere, I need to follow through.

This kind of discipline was not something I was used to growing up. My brother and I didn't have responsibilities requiring any kind of discipline. Chaos filled my childhood home, and when insanity is on the daily menu, basics take a back seat. Looking back, I realized my parents didn't care about my welfare. I didn't even brush my teeth every day because I never learned it was important. The only times growing up I heard about teeth was when someone was yelling about having to go to the dentist, pay a dental bill, or was suffering from a tooth ache. The principle there was to deal with teeth when there became a problem or an inconvenience. I know now (and most people do) that by maintaining good dental health, the problems are so much less.

Ironically, each and every tooth in my mouth grew loose and threatened to fall out thanks to my Scleroderma. In 2014, I saw four different dentists and periodontists to figure out what to do with my loose teeth. Many wanted to pull each tooth and replace them with dentures or a new set of implants. I was not ready to do this and would not stop until I found a solution that did not include pulling all my natural teeth. I found a great implant dentist, and today I still have *almost* all my teeth and a smile from ear to ear.

In 1985, another opportunity appeared for me to learn discipline, follow through, and commitment, and I see now what an incredible gift that was. Every Monday night at 6:30, I volunteered to help at a meeting. It was my job to set up chairs, get the coffee ready, and greet people as they arrived. They counted on me to be there, and I was committed to this for an entire year.

Being there made me happy because it was a place with wonderful people who helped me maintain sanity in my life and kept me going in the right direction. Having others depend on me taught me a new discipline I had lacked up to that point in my life. When I showed up and took care of my responsibilities, they acknowledged it, approved of it, and complimented me for it. Like a puppy getting a stroke on the head, I wanted more. It was unconditional love I hadn't experienced, and I couldn't get enough. Out of the 52 meetings, I only missed two, and 30-plus years later, I can still remember why I missed those two times. Once was because I was in the hospital, and the other was for a vacation out of town.

This same drive and level of commitment is what kept me alive while I laid on the couch and repeated to myself *I'm not going to die. I will get up.* It is what gave me the strength to go to my garden each day and pick two weeds before collapsing back on my sectional, satisfied I accomplished something.

Now, as the CEO of a company with two dozen+ employees, I need to be even more disciplined. People rely on me to run the business effectively, so they have money to pay their mortgages. Paying the bills on time, showing up to work when I am supposed to, making the right choices for the future of the business, and keeping things running smoothly are my responsibilities. If I let those slip, it affects them all. That is a huge responsibility I am happy to carry, but I wouldn't be in this position today if that mentor hadn't shown up in my life to hold me accountable or without my friends at my Monday meeting. They all taught me to suit up, show up, and grow up.

Tough Love

One mentor and strong teacher in my life was Eileen. She came from skid row in Nebraska, where she had lived for a few years at the height of her drinking, and had a rough story. Alcohol took her way down, but she rose from that and made a great life for herself. She came into my life in 1991 and taught me I could be anything I wanted to be. Over time, we started to drift apart; however, her lessons about life never left my mind. In the late 1990's, Eileen was back in my life when she mentored the woman who was my primary mentor at that time. I enjoyed getting to reconnect with her, as a result, for a few years before the turn of the century.

She eventually moved to California, and we drifted apart again. Then around 2004, when I started to get really sick, I sought her out. I needed a strong person who wouldn't focus on my tears and feel sorry for me, but who would listen to what was behind those tears and still tell me what action I needed to take. I needed Eileen. A few weeks after I began my search, I found out she was going to be in my state for a weekend event. I met with her and shared that I was in trouble with a new disease that was trying to kill me, and I needed her help. She happily stepped into that role of my mentor once again, thank God.

One day when I was feeling down, I called her.

"They are getting ready to put me on chemo, and I don't know if I can handle it. My hair is going to fall out, and I am going to feel miserable."

"Well, honey," she said. "What's the alternative?"

"I guess I can continue dying on the couch," I said.

"Is that what you want?" she asked.

"No," I said.

"How much do you like your hair?"

She helped me see the same situation through a new pair of glasses. She wasn't dismissing what I was feeling but directed me to step back and look at it differently. Her comment, "How much do you like your hair?" rings through my mind on a regular basis even today. It resets my expectations and fears from that hard but simple question. It was, after all, just hair.

She taught me, time and again, to look at my circumstances through a logical set of eyes rather than feeling sorry for myself. To let go of self-pity and replace it with gratitude and determination. She loved me with every part of her being, but she put I over E—intellect over emotion. She would always say to me, "I don't care how you are feeling. What are you doing to improve the situation?"

Life isn't always easy, and there are times we need to move past the feelings and go into action. She wanted to remind me of that. I don't have to want to be at work to still show up. There are no college classes for this kind of learning.

Over the years, different mentors came into my life and even though in my mind I questioned what they were asking me to do, I would respond with, "Yes, ma'am." I trusted them to guide me in the right direction. The principles that got me to stop drinking and to stay alive when I became sick all came from the love of these strong women.

CYA (Cover Your Ass)

As a young adult, I found different people just like me, "strays" who either needed some direction or had fallen on harder times and felt down and out. I was honored and privileged enough to be invited into their lives, to help, and take care of them. By doing this, I felt needed, valued, and like I mattered. In 2010, when I started MenuTrinfo®, I found a whole new part of the world to nurture. I took my passion for helping others and figured out how to make it into a business serving the dining public across the country. It allowed me a way to have a positive impact on people across the country by educating and teaching those in the restaurant industry about how to safely handle food and be of service to those with food allergies.

When a particle as small as a speck can kill an allergic 12-year-old, that's a big deal. Taking what I had learned about food allergies, I used it to create our training program with the help of others in the industry. The ingredients for the training program are the same exact ones I use for many areas throughout my life—ask for help, find ways to get my own education on a subject, and surround myself with amazing people that are like-minded and who also want to help others. Our training now contains the necessary information to change the way a chef prepares a meal for a young adult at college or how a restaurant handles a person with special dietary needs.

I didn't receive a formal schooling or a degree in food safety, but I did learn and become an expert on this subject. I became a food safety trainer with other programs. I studied what was available in the industry, at that time in 2010, to help others. Now I have this position and responsibility to provide the correct numbers and information to our clients. People's health and even lives depend on it, and I take that responsibility extremely seriously.

For the nutrition side of our company, our clients are restaurant owners, brand convenience-stores, theme parks, movie theaters, and just about any place you can buy a meal today. When we provide them the nutrition information about their menus, it affects their customers as well. We impact approximately 10 million people each and every day. That's a long way from the couch.

We work with a large fried fish chain based out of the South with over 500 locations. Over the past four years, they hired us for nutrition information and advice. They love us, and we love them. They ask us the questions that their consumers ask them. We take pride in providing them the right answers which then get passed on down to their customers.

That's a lot of responsibility because if our information is wrong, there might be dire consequences for people with allergies. But rather than freak out or lose it, the first thing I did when I started the business was hire a lawyer and the second was to get the right insurance. This lesson of CYA (cover your ass) is an important one every business owner should take seriously. Make sure you have the right insurance, the right attorney, the right contracts, but don't run away from the responsibility.

Other businesses in my field put hundred percent of the responsibility onto the clients to check boxes for allergens and provide software the clients have to use themselves. With our software, when we enter in a recipe, we identify the allergens in the meal. Our competitors make the restaurant owner add that info. How is that helping? How is that being accurate? You're either going to own or you won't. We own it. In 8+ years, it's never come back to bite me in the butt. If it does, I am prepared.

Play to Your Strengths

Every person has different skills. I am a great salesperson who can sell a drowning man water and get him to buy a second cup. It might be because I was trained to manipulate during my childhood in order to take care of myself, so I developed this character trait, or it was because I was just born with the skill. Regardless, I am very good at quickly reading people and sizing up a situation to mirror back what they want. I have discovered that being able to read an audience makes me an effective public speaker as well.

Being a gifted salesperson is a rare skill, so after slinging drinks for a while in my 20s, I went back to doing what I do best—sales. I sold pre-plated school lunches from Maryland to Maine, selling over 8 million dollars' worth of products each year. As a mover and shaker, I had a blast. If you love what you are doing, it will never feel like work. That's how it felt back then, and that is how it feels now. I love what I am doing.

Now that I run my own company, I use this with my employees as well. It is important to me they enjoy their job. To do this, I need to make sure I put them in a position that plays to their strengths. If someone enjoys working on the computer, but doesn't like talking on the phone, I wouldn't place her in an administrative assistant position where she answers phones and greets people when they come to the office. Instead, I would assign her to something computer focused and look for someone who is a people person for the admin position.

Passing It On

Since the inception of my company, I have run it with passion and a commitment to creating a culture of community and teamwork with the employees. When they first start working for us, they don't always embody the same drive I do, but the ones who stick around eventually get there.

There is a leader here who works in the nutrition division. She loves it and feels nutrition is where she belongs. But every time an AllerTrain™ manager leaves, this employee steps into that role until I can hire a new manager. She knows how to do the job. She has been here 3 ½ years, and she is a rock star at it. I believe her strong and determined attitude comes from all her years playing sports. It has been a gift to watch it emerge from her at work, since she didn't possess it when I first hired her. Now, I am confident when she steps into this temporary role that nothing will fall through the cracks.

I am preparing to be out of the office in 2018 for a number of months to have an intense stem cell procedure done for my scleroderma and will be away for a while. I called her into my office.

"One of my fears in leaving for a few months is that I don't have a new AllerTrain™ manager yet," I said. "You're the acting manager, and I know you want to go back to nutrition. What are your thoughts on this?"

She looked me straight in the eye and said, "I will do anything you need, for as long as you need it. I won't leave Aller-Train™ until you find a replacement who I can train."

We have hired a new manager in that role, and she has benefited from the team spirit that has been shown to her as she gets settled in her new position.

This is somebody taking on the passion I have and the determination to suit up and show up to do what is needed. She takes it to a whole new level. I wish she would stay in the position permanently, but she doesn't love it. It's not her jam, and I want to honor that and not force my will down her throat. If I want to keep her as an employee, I need to respect her wishes and allow her to do the job she loves. She is fine stepping in when needed because she knows I will eventually let her go back to what she enjoys most, nutrition. She will be happy and fulfilled there in what she's doing. That's good for my business and good for her mental health, both of which matter to me.

Be a Good Model

As CEO, I have the chance to educate the dozen young women who work in my office and model for them the principles in this book. When I see one of my team leaders use a principle that I have been modeling, and use it with their team members or clients, it makes me proud.

We had a customer that came to us and needed nutritionals done in two weeks so they could get a use and occupancy in New York to open a new restaurant. If an establishment has 20 or more locations, it must have a menu with calorie counts on it. It doesn't matter what the federal law says, that's the mandate in Long Island, New York.

We were in the middle of a huge crunch in the nutrition department. At this time, nutritionals were taking anywhere from 6-10 weeks. We had to input all the recipes and ingredients from the restaurant's menu into our system in order to create those. I called our nutrition director, Claire.

"We have this opportunity to help a client," I told her. "We can charge a little extra to expedite it. Do you think we can do it?"

Claire said, "I don't see why not."

This is the spirit and the attitude (and passion) I bring to the business and something I love to see in my employees. For five years, right out of college, Claire has worked with me. She has adopted these same principles and uses them every day. It is the kind of spirit that changes how America eats and the kind that changes a company.

She and her team worked twenty-four seven for two solid weeks and delivered the nutritionals to the client on day 13. Nothing stopped them from getting it done. We received extra money for the quick turnaround, and I told her I'd like to pass on a bonus to her, to divide up among herself and her team as a thank you. I gave Claire a number and told her to split it up based on how she saw fit. She gave me back a little three-inch sticky Post-it note. On it were four people's names and how much she was giving them. She divided it evenly among those names, but the one name missing was hers.

I said, "I can do this, Claire, but your name is not on here. What's going on?"

She looked at me and said, "I'm doing a Betsy. Will you let me?"

I smiled at her, and my eyes filled with tears.

"I most certainly will."

She didn't want any of the extra money. She only wanted to give it to her team that worked so hard. That's passion, and when you combine it with a focused purpose, the results are incredible. That's teaching a young lady how to be a strong leader.

The Money Will Come

One thing I learned on my own, that I wish somebody would have told me seven years ago, was that the money will come, but only if you pay close attention. Before starting the business, I barely knew how to balance a checkbook. I made myself read money magazines, read blogs, and work with a business-savvy mentor. Now, I am super-hyper-crazy-vigilant about my financial reports, such as the profit and loss statements (P&L) and balance sheets, to name a couple.

One piece of advice for every business owner and entrepreneur is know every penny or you won't have any. It's that simple. Education in this area is not optional at all; it is mandatory. I can tell you right now exactly how much is owed to us, where we are with P&L for the month, where we are with P&L for the year, what money is coming in, and what I have concerns about.

I won't lease an office space without knowing I can cover it. I won't hire anyone if I am not 100% sure I can pay their salary. We are a cash business. Except for the office space, I own everything related to the company, down to the folding chairs we use for meetings. I have a saying I abide by every day, "Never write a check with my mouth my ass can't cash." If I can't pay for something, I won't financially commit to it.

To be successful in business, you need to know and understand your financial status. You need to know what your money is doing. There are many resources available to read. You can contact your local small business development center to see if there are classes or find a successful business person to be your mentor. Creating financial stability for you and your business is at the core of your recipe for long term success.

My new challenge with money these days is taking time to enjoy some of it. Profit is NOT a dirty word but not allowing myself to enjoy the fruits of my labor would be a shame. I need to take some for myself and enjoy it to the fullest.

Lead with Love and Kindness

Back in 1992, I had a restaurant client in Annapolis, Maryland named Chick and Ruth's. During one visit, the owner, a great man named Chick, said to me, "It costs you nothing to be nice. Always lead with kindness." This idea was new to me, and I wanted to figure out how to live that saying. It had such an impact on me.

From that point on, using love and kindness in business has been a number one goal of mine. Although there are many days I fall short, believe me, I try my best. The company, as a whole, holds the core values of honesty, integrity, and service, but underlying every one of these is the foundation of love or kindness. You don't hear many business speakers talking about love from the front of the room, but I think if you come from a place of love, nothing but goodwill will follow.

If you ask me why I have been able to start and run a successful business, in a brand-new space in an established industry, changing the way the restaurant business does things, it all stems from love and kindness. This includes how a training is going to look, how we are going to take care of our nutrition clients, how I treat my employees, or how I treat myself. It all comes from that core center.

In the business world, we aren't cheerleaders enough for each other. We are too competitive. Many are too scared and think *I am not going to get mine if we work together.* But I found that if I help you get yours, I always get mine. It just seems to appear. That's kindness. That's what Chick told me.

This idea carries over into my emails too. It is rare I don't say something like, "you rock," "you are awesome," or "you are amazing." Some people think I am full of crap, and I am trying to be overly sweet. They may also say that as the CEO, I should maintain a more professional image. But people do blow me away, and I want them to know it.

Years ago, someone introduced me to a guy on LinkedIn who is a thought leader. He is way ahead of his time with his ideas and is brilliant. He is a super successful businessman who happens to be a gazillionaire.

He has been nothing but kind to me. Our relationship has benefited me tremendously. He sent me a text recently letting me know my name came up positively in a conversation, and he wanted me to know. He constantly thinks of others. It's just amazing.

Nurturing Office Environment

Taking care of people is in my nature and some days more so then others. In general, I believe women are hardwired to nurture more than men. It is in my DNA to decide in the morning what will we have for dinner that evening. Most men, at least the three I have been married to, don't think the same way first thing in the morning. Eventually, in the evening, they think *Hey what's up for dinner?* By then, I already have a plan.

When I started the company, I was a new empty nester. With my daughter grown up and on her own and my step son also out of the house, there was no one home to take care of anymore. As the business grew, and I added an office space and employees, that changed.

Initially, I tried so hard not to act like a mother to all these young 20-year-olds coming out of college to work for the different branches of MenuTrinfo®. Business books said *Don't do that.* It was not my job to take care of the employees to that level, even though they were the same age as my daughter. This guidance felt staunch, but I assumed there must be something to it since I was still new to this kind of role.

Part of taking care of people is wanting to feed them. Providing snacks for my staff was a way I could do this. But that voice in my head said that if I did this, then it would look like I was trying to be their mom, and that's not what CEOs do. This was one of those times I told that inside voice to shut up and sent it to the corner. It wasn't needed. There was nothing wrong with buying snacks for these young men and women who worked their butts off for me.

You can walk into the office any day and pick from dozens of different snacks. My employees love them, and I love buying them. Our work environment is supportive, encouraging, and nurturing. It's a place where people work hard, and they are acknowledged for their efforts. I have taken the staff to baseball games, treated them to a spa day after a big project is completed, included their loved ones in group activities wherever possible, gone bowling, painting, and hosted pot luck lunches (free from gluten and the big eight food allergies), and of course, the snacks.

What I learned is I could be a woman and a CEO, and they could go hand in hand. Being a woman didn't make me any less of a CEO, and vice versa, being a CEO makes me no less of a woman. Trusting that woman-ness and trusting that nature allows me to show appreciation to those around me in an appropriate way. And by the way, they do rock.

Wisdom: Food for Thought

➢ Reflect back on all the past mentors in your life. Take a moment to write down all their names and the biggest lesson you learned from each of them.

➢ Who are the current mentors in your life? Write down their names and why they are important to you.

➢ Over the next few weeks, if possible, reach out to these mentors from your past and present and let them know how much you appreciate them.

➢ List your top five strengths related to your career or business.

➢ Reflect on the ways you are using those strengths. Can you be using them more?

➢ In this chapter, I talk about the importance of knowing where every penny goes. Whether you own your own business or work for someone else, you should know what is happening with your money. On a scale of 1 to 10 (one being the lowest), rate yourself on your knowledge of your financial matters. If it is not a 10, make a list of the steps you are going to take to improve that.

CHAPTER 9

Value Your Work

Spiritual Principle: Honesty

hon·es·ty (noun) truthfulness, sincerity, or frankness.

When I talk about a "recipe for success" to a large group or one on-one, the key components I mention are the ingredients that come in the form of the principles I have been sharing with you and the directions on how to mix them all together to create the perfect result for a successful business and a happy and joyous life.

Out of all the principles, honesty is the one I see as the foundation that holds it all together. Like the way eggs bind cake batter, this principle is essential for success.

When I started MenuTrinfo®, I took three of my own personal core beliefs and applied them to the foundation of the company: honesty, integrity, and service. These are the primary values all our decisions are based on with honesty being at the center. For some, there can be gray areas, but for me it is black and white—you are either honest, or you aren't. I run my company and my life from a place of truthfulness. It's not always easy because honest conversations can sometimes be uncomfortable, but it is the right way to approach situations.

Be Honest, Not Mean

I remember Eileen teaching me to "Say what you mean, mean what you say, and try not to say it mean." At times, that can be a tall order. It leaves little room for misunderstanding, and shared in the right spirit, it can be a shortcut to accomplishing the goal for the conversation. In my health that goal was simple, not die. In business, the goal got a little more complicated with clients, partners, financial reports, bottom lines, HR, and deliverables, but none the less, it was always there.

Much of my younger years were spent living in that gray area between truth and lies. During childhood, it wasn't so much about blatant lies but more of sweeping things under the rug and pretending they didn't exist. Lying through omission was an everyday occurrence. As an eight-year-old, when I fell asleep at bedtime, I didn't know if I would be allowed to sleep through the night or if my father was going to slam into my room, in the pitch dark, screaming for me to get up and talk to him. Apparently, he didn't like to be alone when drunk in the wee, small hours of the night, and I was his go-to sounding board.

I would wake up, sit next to him on the side of my bed, and let him talk, sob, babble on and use me as his company. The middle of the night conversations could last for minutes or hours. Whatever it took to make him feel better. Listening to this grown man, who I was supposed to respect, slobber and slur all over himself in a drunken stupor did not make me respect him; it made me scared. Many years later, he did apologize, but the underlying lessons learned, the feelings I experienced, and the memories never went away. I can and did forgive him, but I have never forgotten. However, I digress, let me get back to how this effects my relationship with the truth.

During those nights I kept my father company, I knew the minute he walked through the door that my next day at school was going to be tough. I was not allowed to tell anyone what was happening at home. It was a family secret, kept in the dark. Getting up for school, trying to stay awake, to be focused, and to learn become my mission at a very young age. Wiping sleep from my eyes, I told anyone that asked how I was doing that I was fine. All was well, I was just having a hard time focusing. Some days, all I wanted to do was disappear and sleep all day. When I could get my hands on alcohol, I would use it as an escape, and I did feel like I could disappear with it. My grades in school were never great, and this was one reason why.

It became a problem for me because I did not have an off switch. Lying at a young age about what happened in my home late at night was the beginning of dishonesty in my life. First, covering for others, then covering for me. This became my norm through my teenage years. It was far from honesty or the truth, but it was the truth I was allowed to tell.

#MeToo [1]

In middle school, I had been molested at school by two young boys over a period of a couple months. They took liberties to grab at me, pull on me, and make horribly inappropriate comments to me anytime they felt like it. I finally reached my breaking point and couldn't take it anymore. One day, they did something to me, and I jumped up on a table in our wood working/metal shop classroom and started screaming. I used loud, colorful language to try to protect myself and finally got the

---

[1] Tarana Burke, founder of a nonprofit that helps survivors of sexual violence, created the Me Too movement in 2006 to encourage young women to show solidarity with one another. In 2017, the hashtag #MeToo went viral and became a rallying cry against sexual assault and harassment.

attention of an adult. The teacher listened as I shared what happened in his classroom but also about what had been happening in the halls, playground, lunchroom, and anywhere these two wanted to torment me. The teacher sprang into action. The local police were called, and the boys were pulled from school.

When I got home later, my mother stood in the front hallway and said, "Go upstairs and shower. We are never talking about this again. It didn't happen." And she walked down the hall. That was it. We never did talk about it again. What they did was wrong, and what they did to me as an innocent, sweet middle schooler was wrong. But the fact that I wasn't allowed to talk about it was also wrong. That was just the next level of lying through omission. It was the beginning of my #metoo story that is a very sad tale for a different book. The lying and covering up I learned here was massive and continued until it was mandatory for me to get honest in all areas of my life to get and stay sober.

These kinds of secrets are like the nasty mold growing in the corner of your shower. Instead of dealing with it by replacing the grout, Clorox is poured over, the stain goes away for a little while, eventually resurfacing stronger and more determined to stay. By pretending a problem isn't there doesn't help the issue. Eventually, the mold comes through. I don't care who you are, it comes through.

Moment of Truth

With alcohol, I had to quit lying to myself and stop believing that I was dependent on and addicted to alcohol, that I needed it to function. I had to face the facts that I was running my life into the ground, and the only way to fix it was to drop drinking. Completely. Friends stepped up to help me and hold me accountable, but ultimately it was up to me to maintain that honesty. If they asked me if I had a drink, I needed to be truthful, regardless of whether the answer was yes or no.

Honesty took on an entirely new importance to me after I started my new journey of not drinking. I had to take it one day at a time. If I wanted to put a life together worth living—one that could and would include joy, laughter, freedom, happiness, and rewards—it could only be done with honesty at the foundation. It was the base ingredient in my recipe for my new life. Everything else branched off of this.

It has been over 30 years since I have had a drink. I never expected it to last this long. I frequently say that had I known my last drink was in fact, my last one, I probably would have had one or two more as a final goodbye. This type of thinking explains why I am someone who should never drink.

Because of my business being part of the restaurant industry, I get to attend lots of dinners and events where alcohol flows as a natural part of the function. Interestingly enough, it is just part of the meals, evenings, and activities, and it is no big deal for 99% of the folks that attend. For me, it is also no big deal to be around it, and I am completely fine with choosing not to partake.

I remember many nights going out with my all-time favorite Master Chef in the industry. This man is a serious legend for his accomplishments as a chef, an educator, and now as a mentor to so many others. He is well respected in the industry, and the mention of his name makes folks stand a little straighter. The people serving us want this chef to eat their best food and enjoy it with the best paired wines. Of course, as a guest at the table with this amazing chef, I am offered wine, but I simply smile and say no thanks. Then I get to sit and appreciate the company of all the other guests while enjoying my iced tea and the great conversation. If someone does ask why I am not drinking the wine, I say, "You know what, I've had my drinks. I'm good."

There is usually a nod of acceptance, and we get on with the great evening. It is not a big deal. I love my life today without alcohol influencing it.

When I apply the principle of honesty in this area of my life, it is easy to see I can be honest while not being a "joy killer." I don't need to lay my past out on the table for everyone to inspect or go into details of my life. There is no need to apologize for who I am or who I was. I can be honest in my actions and stay true to myself. I look at it and think about the bigger picture in our society about the honesty of that. There is no need to manipulate that or lie about that. I am who I am, and that comes through my actions even if someone can't hear my words.

Getting Honest with Myself

Raw, real, gut level honesty was what I needed to face and decide what to do with the death sentence I was given, thanks to my Scleroderma. Living in denial was no longer an option. I remember thinking how angry I was for the bluntness of how I was told my life was going to come to a quick end. As I thought through it more, I wondered, how else could she have told me? What would have softened the blow? In reality, it was the type of truth I personally appreciated once the fingermarks faded from the emotional face slap. It allowed me to take the worst-case scenario, process it, then make a plan. This kind of direct approach helped me then and still works for me today. It's the half-truths and beating around the bush BS that makes me CRAZY!

All I had to do at that time was look down at my fingers, which I could barely move, and stare at my cold, hard face in the mirror to see the skin had become so tight it looked like I was riding 75 mph on a motorcycle without a helmet. My physical shape had gone from normal to nice and round, thanks to medications, immobility, and fear. Pain surged through me on a daily basis. I could hardly function.

Knowing I was a ticking time bomb changed my frame of reference and outlook rapidly. I realized sitting on the couch feeling sorry for myself, my circumstances, and my lot in life was not an option for me if I planned to live. Being sick on the couch opened my eyes and shined spotlights on the areas of my life I needed to change. It was time to get real and lose the underlying anger I still carried from my childhood. I began to look back and see those childhood incidents as sad, but I no longer had to lie about them or invest time and energy into them.

It was during this time I took a long hard, honest look at my role in all of this. I refer to this time as my "Come to Jesus" chat with myself. I had to pay attention to what foods I put in my body and make better choices. My focus in life needed to shift away from thoughts of myself to thoughts of others. It took an intervention from God and honest self-reflection to cause a spirit of strength to rise from somewhere deep inside of me and move me toward becoming a successful business owner.

Tell the Doctors the Truth

I am all about telling the truth, but for some reason when it came to my health care during the early years of being sick, that was not the case. I wasn't flat out lying to the doctors, but I wasn't telling them the whole truth. If they gave me a medication that didn't work, I felt if I was completely honest it would somehow hurt their feelings. So I wouldn't tell them everything about how the drugs were or were not affecting me. Somewhere in my mind I justified this because I thought I was sparing them the disappointment of learning what they gave me wasn't helping.

When I finally took a step back and remembered this was a fight for my life, it became clear that I needed to be 100% honest with doctors, regardless of how I thought it would make them feel and vice versa. It was up to me to be the driver of my recovery. If I felt they were not reciprocating that truthfulness or were shuffling me through treatments, but not fully invested in my healing, I fired them and moved on. I didn't have time to waste with practitioners who didn't believe I could get better. Finding a doctor who listened to me and allowed me to be an active part of my recovery became my top priority.

I had no intention of dying and planned to fight and scrap as hard as I could in order to live. Staying honest with myself and those helping me was necessary and became an integral part of my story and how I ended up going from the couch and death's door to running a million-dollar nutrition company.

Honesty in the Office

With me, what you see is what you get. My employees understand this and know I will always be honest with them. Around the office, I share a lot with them. They know about my husband and my daughter, and I am very open about my scleroderma. It's my personality and who I am. I consider the folks in my office family. That being said, I am still running a company, and I am their boss. I can be friendly and approachable, but I need to keep that line clear between CEO and employee. There are boundaries and aspects of my life that I don't disclose. It isn't because I am trying to hide something or be dishonest, but not everything is appropriate to share at the office.

As a CEO, there are times when I need to have tough conversations with the people in the office. It might be about their performance, an interaction with a client, or an issue with the company. Regardless of how uncomfortable the chat goes, I always approach it with honesty and frankness. Because of this, I have the same expectation from my employees.

When I find employees stretching the truth, omitting information, or faking denial on something, I make it clear to them I understand what the truth is, and they are not being 100% truthful. I have already invested time in hiring and training them. I don't think it makes a lot of sense to show them to the door for these things. But I don't think there is any benefit to the health of the company to pretend it didn't happen. There is a thin line between stretching truth and a blatant lie.

At our company, I call it our zero tolerance for lies. When I hire someone to join our team, I tell them up front during the interview process that if they are caught in a lie, they will be fired immediately. When an employee lies to me or another member of the team, it makes them untrustworthy in my eyes. People teach and tell me who they are through what they say and their actions. It is 100% my job to believe them. If what they are saying and doing is dishonest, I tend to believe them as I help them find the door.

What my company does on a daily basis, by supplying nutritional information and even through our trainings, impacts people's lives and health. On any given day, 2.5-3 million people in the country use our information and rely on it to be accurate. For some, it is a matter of life and death. It is imperative we approach everything we do with honesty and integrity. There is no room for cutting corners of any kind and lying. Our mission is to protect lives and health. A lie in our business can kill someone. Because of this, I only keep employees around who understand the scope of what we do.

Sick Time

I didn't go the grad school, MBA route, so sometimes I am unsure what I am "supposed to" do in certain business situations. Instead, I rely on my basic principles to guide me. Our mission statement says we protect people's lives and health. This applies to not only our clients and the folks who rely on the accuracy of our nutritional information, but for me, it includes the people in our office. So, when it comes to honesty and sick days, I have a policy that may not be the "norm" in other companies, but it works for me and supports our own mission.

Every employee gets one week of sick time. I trust them to be honest about this and use these when they are ill. It is not fair to anyone in the office if someone knows they are coming down with something and they show up to work anyway (this includes me). If I find out, I will send them home. If they are showing up because they have used up their sick days, then I will add time for them. It is important that the office maintains a healthy environment where all the employees can trust that those who are sick will stay home. Since we are all about protecting lives and health, it would be wrong for me to have people working in the office who are ill.

Honesty with Clients

There have been times when I have had to enforce my 100% honesty policy with clients. We had a client who we actually fired because he wanted us to fudge their numbers. This gentleman, who was part of a national restaurant chain, came to us. He knew some of our other clients and wanted to hire us because of our accuracy with our numbers. We ran his recipes through our system, and his numbers came out awful. His recipes had never been looked at through the glasses of nutrition, and they came out looking very unhealthy. The meals served at his locations were more about spoiling yourself with amazing food and not worrying about the ingredients.

He tried everything he could to get us to manipulate the data, so it would look more favorable on his menu.

He asked, "Can't you call it a half of portion?"

"Can't you cut out that item?"

Every time we stayed with the letter of the law, as mandated by the FDA, he pushed back and tried to get us to alter the numbers. Of course, we weren't going to do that. He became such a pain because he wouldn't take *no* for an answer. This went on for about six months. He became frustrated with us because we wouldn't do what he wanted, and we knew we couldn't do what he was asking and keep our core values. We went above and beyond for him, giving him more reports than we normally give folks, so he would have everything he needed when he left. We are never happy to see a client go, but in the end, we had to walk away. I don't ever want revenue if it is dishonest. It was an easy decision to make, but a sad one.

You Are Your Brand

Whether we like it or not, the people who make up a company, from the CEO to the employees, represent that business' brand. If they are doing something shady or dishonest in their personal life, it can reflect poorly on the business. My goal is to live an honest life, both at work and at home; there is no separation. A truly trustworthy person maintains that value regardless of the situation.

How I present myself at home, in the office, and in the community, reflects on my business and the brand I created. It is up to me to decide what I want that image to be. Sharing my story of sickness and my journey to better health has been one of the coolest parts of this hard walk. Letting others see my truth, even when it's not pretty, has been a beacon for others to know they are not alone on their journeys. That matters to me.

What Are Your Services Really Worth?

There is a trust on the part of clients or customers when they seek out a product or service. They want to believe that what is presented and offered is accurate. Problems happen when a company isn't completely honest with their information. Think of a stereotypical used-car salesman. We get an image of someone exaggerating the good qualities of the car and not mentioning the flaws. We also wonder if we are getting a fair price. This is not the type of impression you want to leave your customers or clients. Of course, you want to be assertive and confident in your product or service, but it should be done with honesty.

On the flip side, a subtler dishonesty can occur when we under-value our product or service. Maybe it's a new business, and we lack that needed confidence, so we second-guess our pricing and the value. Potential customers will pick up on this, and it may leave them feeling unsure about what we are offering.

When I first started MenuTrinfo®, I had very little idea how to price, value, or offer our services and products. In time, as my knowledge and confidence grew, it became clearer to me. Today, I don't mind being the more expensive solution because I can say in all honesty we are the better, more accurate, truthful, and sought after outsourced nutritional solution available. Our job is to continue to be that, stay relevant, and be on the cutting edge of the industry.

It doesn't matter what your business is, how many employees you have, or if you are on your own, you need to be confident in your services or product and honest about their value.

Honesty: Food for Thought

➤ Are there areas in your life where you have been lying to yourself? Reflect on why you are doing this and how can you change it.

➤ Recall a time when you had the courage to be completely honest and respectful with someone about a situation. How did you feel after?

➤ You don't have to own a company to have a "brand." In whatever field you work in, how you carry yourself represents your own personal brand and how people at work and in the community see you. What are three things you do to represent a positive personal brand?

➤ Take a few minutes to reflect on your view of yourself at work and think about how much value you bring. Do you tend to undervalue your contributions or services? If so, what changes can you make to fix that?

CHAPTER 10

Keep Your Friends Close and Competitors Closer

Spiritual Principle: Unity

u·ni·ty (noun) a condition of harmony

There's a spiritual law that says we are all equal. Men among men, women among women. It's the spiritual principle of being united as one. If I come from a place of unity with my peers in the restaurant industry, then we are all on the same level. Regardless of title, no one is above or below anyone else. With this mindset, it is easier to support one another and reach out for help from others in our field, including C-level executives, if that is what needs to happen. As a young adult, some of my friends reinforced this idea when they reminded me that every single person goes to the dentist because we all have teeth. Bill Gates has teeth just like I do. I might have more cavities, but our teeth are all basically the same. When Bill Gates gets a toothache and I get a toothache, we will both experience pain. He is not exempt from pain because he is a gazillionaire. He is a person, just like me.

Like many children in our country, I was raised with a strong *us versus them* mentality. It's where the keeping up with the Jones' comes into play in our society. I was taught to never rely on anyone else. Take what I can, when I can, because there might not be enough for everyone. It was more about chaos than togetherness.

When I became sober and hung around a new set of friends who lived life through the type of spiritual principles I have been sharing, my life changed. I experienced a true fellowship and unity in my 20's that I hadn't felt before. The focus of these new relationships was based on support and helping each other the best we could. I learned that working with others, instead of against them, had a positive pay off. Up until then, I wouldn't have believed that to be true.

When I started to get busy with the company, I realized unity needed to be at the core. My focus, and that of my employees, had to be the same. There is a great business writer out there, Simon Sinek. He has a book, *Start with Why*. It helps business owners figure out the Why of what they are doing. This is something my investor/mentor worked with me to understand. He helped me figure out the "why" behind Menu-Trinfo®: we protect people's lives and health. Everything we do stems from this—every single thing. Whether that is providing nutrition information, allergen information, allergen training, or allergen audits, we protect lives and health.

During one training, I stood in the front of a room talking to 42 chefs, all of whom were not happy to be there because their boss signed them up. My mission was to teach them about food allergies and change their eye rolls into compassionate feelings, even when they are slammed and "in the weeds" on a Saturday night. Once I did that, then we were all united. I knew they were going to go out and do right for those people with food allergies. Now they were protecting lives and health also. I made *my* mission *their* mission. That's unity.

There is an awesome chef in a leadership food and beverage role in a casino in Las Vegas. He took an AllerTrain™ training from me in 2012. He had a passion for it and put the Aller-Train™ principles to work in his casino food service. A couple of years ago, he was nominated as food safety person of the year in the state because of what he had done with food allergies. I am not here to say that I changed him or to take credit for all his hard work. But I do think AllerTrain™ was a piece of the puzzle, along with others along the way who had the same goal to protect people.

Let Me Help You

When I started my company, I did not want to come from a place of fear—the idea that someone might steal my idea if I talked to them about it. This sort of paranoia is common throughout my industry, and I am sure it is apparent in others as well. People become scared that they won't get their share of the pie. The truth is, and it is worth reiterating, when I help you get yours, I get mine. That's what makes the unity pie work so well. There is a spiritual outcome that has been evident throughout my life in the last decade or more that has shown me this is true.

In 2011, I created our AllerTrain™ training program with the help of many folks around the country. At that time, the largest trade association in our industry, with over 40,000 members representing nearly 500,000 foodservice establishments, did not have a program like ours. Of course, I wanted them to learn all about mine, to see how well-organized and effective it was so they would want to use it.

In 2012, I made an appointment to meet with the executives of this association. With complete confidence in my program, I took my workbook, hopped a plane, and went to Chicago to meet with them face to face.

I was escorted to the huge board room where the head of all the training programs for the association, and a manager right under him, sat in big comfortable office chairs at a large, dark oak table. I had never seen a board room like this; it sure beat the room I worked out of in my basement. I introduced myself, and they told me to help myself to a beverage before we got started as they motioned to the kitchenette off the side. I stuck with water even though the area was stocked with every drink I could imagine consuming.

With only my program workbook in hand, I described our AllerTrain™ class and what made it unique and necessary in our industry. As they looked through the workbook, my rate of speech went from fast to faster. With every turn of a page, it increased one degree. When I was done, I caught my breath and asked them if they were interested in using it.

One exec said he didn't think they would ever offer a training program like this, and if they did, they would come up with something themselves. Basically, they thought the program was pretty cool, but in a very respectful way, they said no thank you. It was almost like they were patting me on the head saying, "Thanks for sharing. Now go about your business." They weren't interested.

In the spirit of unity and my belief that there is plenty to go around, I didn't need to fear our competition. I stayed friendly with the association, and one gentleman in particular. If we were both attending the same trade show, I'd give him a hug and ask about his wife. I was genuinely interested in knowing how he was doing. If we both had time, we would grab dinner together. We'd talk about families, life, and some about work, but it was more about connecting and hanging out.

About a year later, this man reached out to me. "Hey, Betsy. The association decided we do want to develop an allergy training course (not a huge shocker for me). We believe this is best course of action for us now. We value your expertise and experience and want to know if you are interested in coming to Chicago to be part of the job task analysis team as a subject matter expert?"

"My God, yes!" I said. "When do you need me?"

"It will be in a couple of weeks," he said. "We'll pay for your flight and put you up in the hotel."

"That sounds great," I said. "Thanks for reaching out to me. See you soon."

Even though I had my AllerTrain™ program in my briefcase when I left for Chicago, and understood it was the same type of program the association wanted to create, in the interest of unity and harmony, I needed to suit up, show up, and help. I also must be honest, if the leading trade association in my industry was going to create a competing product, I wanted to know what it contained from the inside out. Although they tried to get me to sign a non-disclosure agreement (NDA) for this Job Task Analysis (JTA), I did not, knowing one day I might want to share this story.

For three solid days, I had the honor of being one of ten+ professionals seated around that same huge conference table I had sat at when I pitched my training program, helping this national trade association develop their program. They were going to do this, with or without my help, so why not be a part of it? As a subject matter expert in the field, I had a lot to offer them. More importantly, I was able to ensure the program was done right for food allergy folks across the country.

In the end, this program would be in direct competition with mine, but I wanted my competitors to be the very best they could be because that's the level I strive for. My experience during the three days was amazing, and I felt grateful to be a part of the process. I don't regret a second of it. Plus, while working on this project, I met one of my biggest clients, one of my best customers, and a future partner for my company. It was a great networking event for me and I hope for them as well.

Not long after, they launched their program in direct competition with AllerTrain™ lite. Because of my involvement in its creation, I knew exactly what their program contained. My name is on a class presentation slide and in their course information, along with all the other creators, the last time I looked.

This association is a huge, well-known entity in the restaurant industry. Is it hard to sell against them? You betcha. However, in the industry and this association, I'm still known as the subject matter expert. Recently this group had their big, annual conference in Chicago. They needed a speaker for a session about food allergens, and they called me. I, of course, did it and loved sharing my knowledge once again. I will always choose the we over me. Spiritually, it's about us.

There have been times when we both solicit the same client regarding our training programs, and I don't get the bid. Instead of wallowing in the fact that I lost out on the client, I understand a different, and many times better, opportunity is right around the corner for me.

Although I lost out on some clients to this program, it opened the door for me to take our allergen training course into others. A great example is I lost out on a trade culinary school but picked up a federal prisons system to handle the food service, and in some cases, teach inmates. Those who participate get a certificate stating they went through this accredited class on safe food handling for allergies. Now they have another skill to take with them to restaurants after they are released and are seeking employment.

There is an awesome homeless shelter in DC that uses our course to provide their folks with a new skill set to make them more appealing in the workforce. I want to be able to give people a skill and put them to work. It's a great way to give back and another way to create harmony.

This is how unity can work in business and how I approached this whole situation. I didn't come from a place of fear, where I imagined them making a product big enough to kick our butts. Instead, here we are years later, and we're still head-to-head. It hasn't always been easy. There have been 2 AM moments when I thought *Why did I go help them when I'm competing against them?* But, I can promise you, being in unity is worth it. It's so much easier and gentler on my stomach.

Staying in Touch

There is a nonprofit patient advocacy group based in Philadelphia for those with celiac disease. The group had a gluten-free training program which they believe competed directly with AllerTrain™. I approached them years ago about partnering with me by adding their module into the celiac disease part of our training. This would get their message across inside our training program, but they weren't interested. Once again, I came from a place of unity and stayed friendly with them. Over the years, I kept in touch with their president.

During one business trip, my flight home got delayed following a convention. The VP of Development for this organization was there, and we grabbed dinner together. There was no hidden agenda; it was about connection.

In 2017, I fielded a phone call from their development person, who is now interested in talking about partnering after all these years. They decided their organization should be dedicated to providing advocacy and information for patients, along with developing and funding research, so training was outside their realm. It felt out of line with their mission, and they wanted to step away from that. So they reached out to me.

The conversation wouldn't have happened if I lived in fear every time I saw them. That woman wouldn't have messaged me on that day to ask, "Can we talk?" If I live in fear, then I am not approachable. By staying friendly with my competition and maintaining the mindset that there is plenty to go around, my business will only become stronger. In the end, we still didn't partner but staying open, willing, and able to have this discussion is what I strive for. To date it has not cost me anything to be willing to have partnership (aka unity) with others where and when it makes sense. I am never sure when the timeline is going to be perfect, but I always keep the doors open for discussion.

Today that discussion has stopped, but maybe one day down the road, it will resume again. I will continue to do what I do and keep protecting people through the best training possible in the country. Being true to myself for my motives and missions no matter what.

Office Culture

The staff at the office is amazing. They are like family to me and to each other. We spend hours together every day, so it is no surprise. The result is a unified culture that values hard work, respect, integrity, support, and encouragement. It is not a competitive environment, and we all enjoy working with each other. Of course, some days are more trying than others. Like all families, there are times we may disagree on things, and there may be some trials to work through. But in the end, we always come back to that place of harmony.

Challenges with this incredible workplace arise when I need to hire someone to fill a position. The person needs to have the proper credentials for the job, but they also need to have a personality that is good fit with current employees. Not everyone is a great fit. And for those who are, everyday isn't going to be sunshine and rainbows.

Thanks to my mentor, I have had to take a hard and deep look at hiring, retaining, engaging, and recruiting a few good folks. He told me that if I allowed people to stay within the company who were not a good fit, and they stayed too long, they would take others down with them. Sadly, I have a great example of this.

I had a gal working for us who had a list of things she didn't want to do. None were items she informed me about before she started. They all got uncovered along the way. Like an over indulgent parent, I tried to accommodate, excuse, and reassign this list of items. Man, did that back fire. Eventually, I lost her and another employee as a result of the bad blood. Whose fault was it? It was 100% MINE. No one else could be blamed. I put my own willpower and wanting this to work above everything else and turned a blind eye to the blatant mismatch that was clear to others. It shouldn't have surprised me when this employee quit with no notice, but it did. I was deeply saddened that someone else left too and that I didn't realize I was destroying the foundation of my company's unity by allowing this to continue as long as it did. I should have stepped in a lot sooner. I was stuck in what I refer to as analysis paralysis, hoping if I hung in there long enough, it would all work out. But it never did. It was a huge lesson for me to learn that, unfortunately, cost me one good employee.

In Sickness and in Health

Unity is at the core of a good marriage, and in mine to Rocky, that is very true. My scleroderma made it so he had to be by my side, be my biggest champion, and my true partner in everything. Being married to my best friend, who is also my partner in health and business, is an incredible gift that I don't take for granted.

When I first got sick, we approached it together as a united front. He went to every appointment with me, studied day and night to look for answers, drove me everywhere, and would support me however I needed it. The closest scleroderma support group was 65 miles away, and each month, he happily drove me to the meeting. He was the first to volunteer for a fundraising effort and the one beside me at every chicken dinner event. Sometimes caregivers get pushed to the side, and I never wanted Rocky to feel that way. I make it a point to honor him because I know without him and his support, I would be dead.

He truly understands me and knows my need to be in control whenever possible. When going into appointments with doctors, I tell him how I want to the handle the doctor or a procedure or process. We talk through it, and even if he doesn't agree 100% with the direction I want to go, he still hangs back and allows me to run the show. Although we both understand my desire for control, without him on my team, I'd be going in circles without a clear path to a goal.

Opening myself up to trust someone so deeply was tough at first because I hadn't experienced much of that in my early years growing up. I had to let go of my doubts and simply believe he would follow through. There were many times I was too sick to move, and he was there for me. He has never let me down.

Power in Numbers

In my fight to not let scleroderma kill me, I found kindred spirts with a support group through the Scleroderma Foundation in Denver. I was desperate to connect with people going through the same challenges I was and have the chance to talk with them and help each other. I had no problem making the monthly three-hour round trip if it meant finding that unity through our shared experiences. Going through this disease alone is horrible so finding others to go through it together was a Godsend.

When I first started the support group, I was excited, but they had a lady running it whose son died from scleroderma. Every time we showed up, we had to talk about her son, auto-immune diseases, and family history regarding the disease.

It wasn't working for me. I needed some recovery, some hope. It was empowering to have the unity of being surrounded by people who also had the disease, but I couldn't take another month of this woman prattling on about her son and asking all of us if anyone in our family suffered from arthritis or lupus. I needed to talk about scleroderma, find solutions for dealing with the physical and emotional pain, find out what others were going through, and felt the others in the room wanted that too.

Not one to sit back and whine about the situation, I took action. I reached out to the foundation and asked if I could take over leading the group. They agreed, and I started by reformatting the meeting structure to look more like the meetings I attended when becoming sober. Each month we focused on a different topic, and I would bring in experts to talk with us. It could be a nutritionist talking about food, or a yoga instructor sharing helpful stretches, or a doctor talking with us about Raynaud's which we all suffered from. Then following the talk, we would have a social hour and fellowship. I planned out a year at a time, organizing different events and speakers who could share their expertise. We all started getting more out of the meetings, and we were learning helpful information along with the camaraderie and bonds we formed with each other.

For years I attended (and organized) the meetings for the dozen to two dozen folks who showed up each month. They were a mix of people with scleroderma and caregivers. It worked well and gave me and the others the support needed to cope. Over time, my work schedule started getting busier, so I had to stop attending the support group meetings. I helped with fundraising walks when I could, and I also made myself available on social media for those with the disease who needed someone to connect with.

Being united with others experiencing the same challenges I have has been a tremendous blessing over the years, and I have met some amazing people. I have also lost many dear friends to this nasty disease. Out of the twelve or so people from my original support group who had the disease, there is only me and one other woman left. The others have died. I think of Margo, Cheryl, and Kate, along with the other women. It touches my heart, and I feel blessed to have known them. Their faces cross my mind often, and I wonder *How am I still here?* That's the unstoppable piece. I am not only alive, but I am doing something I love and am making a positive impact on the restaurant industry. It blows my mind when I think about it. And at the same time, I realize what an incredible gift of life I have been given, and I have no intention of wasting it.

Unity in a Mission

Because of the experiences in my 20s when I found a group of people I could trust to help and support me, I saw how being in the middle of a herd was a comfortable place for me. When I began my business, and found a mission I felt passionate about, I knew I needed to reach out to like-minded folks and find my tribe of people—those I could talk to about business, the restaurant industry, menu labeling, and nutrition.

Developing that in business for me was easier because I had to develop that in my life to get sober, then to not die. Looking at all people as equal—men, women, CEOs, managers—made it easy to be unified with others without feeling intimidated or better/worse than anyone else.

I have taken the principle of unity and made it a priority in the business. Competitor or not, I will invite just about anyone to lunch, dinner, or coffee. Regardless of titles, of how intimidating someone appears, or how important they think they are, I want to know them. If I come from a place of getting to know them and not wanting something from them other than friendship, it's easy and creates lifelong relationships.

At an evening industry event at a museum, I had been doing the cocktail party shuffle. Almost every person at the event was a C-level, industry rock star, or someone trying to get the attention of said rock stars. To make the evening more interesting, I decided to make a game out of the event. My goal became to try to learn one work/industry fact about as many people as I could in the two hours left.

As I circulated around, I learned about one CEO's meditation practice, the chemo another was starting the following week, and the type of show dogs a marketing guru called family. One man, a mover and shaker for the industry, told me all about the addiction his son was struggling with and another had been in short term recovery, and I got to be a safe place for him to share and connect that night.

The point is not *what I learned* as much as how I got to connect and *feel unified* in shared knowledge of one another. Many of the other principles feed into unity because it would be difficult to try to create unity without the others, but in combination, they can and will make a person unstoppable. They made me unstoppable.

Unity: Food for Thought

➤ Who are your major competitors in your line of work? Are there ways you can partner with them? Reflect on the benefits of that and what it would take to make that happen.

➤ If you work in an office, what ways do you contribute to making it a positive atmosphere? Is this something you can improve on? If so, what are the ways you can do this?

➤ In this chapter, I talked about the importance of building your tribe, especially with your business or career. Do you have group or individuals you meet with regularly to discuss business related issues?

➤ If not, make a list of people you would like to reach out to or a group you would like to join. What are some steps you can take to make this happen?

CHAPTER 11

Gratitude Has a Place at the Table Everyday

Spiritual Principle: Gratitude

grat·i·tude (noun) quality of being thankful; readiness to show appreciation for and to return kindness.

C oming from a space of gratitude can change your perspective and outlook on life. It causes you to open your eyes and notice the good things happening all around you. It doesn't mean there won't be challenges, but they are no longer the focus. Your attention falls on what you do have instead of what you don't. Whether it has been in my business or personal life, whatever I focus on grows. If my attention is on what I lack, then I will never feel as though I have enough. On the flip side, when I celebrate the abundance in my life, I will always feel satisfied and that abundance will continue to flourish.

When I first started my company and worked from my basement, I had two choices. I could complain about not having enough money for a "real" office, or I could be grateful that we had extra room in our house for me to have a temporary work space. I chose to be thankful, and it served me well. My basement served its purpose until I needed to hire more employees. Then, after acquiring a few key clients, I had the money to rent an office and begin building my staff. With each step, I felt gratitude and appreciated where the business was at that time. Of course, it was my intention to continue to build the business and look toward the future, but there is a difference between looking ahead because you are unsatisfied with the current situation or being grateful where you are now but still planning the future. Gratitude keeps your mind centered on what matters the most and enables you to be open to new opportunities that may come your way.

Attitude of Gratitude

For some people, making a shift to an attitude of gratitude may come easy. For me, it was a gradual shift that began when I decided to become sober. Up until then, my life felt veiled by childhood secrets. I had been taught to not trust anyone, and everything I did focused on what was in it for me. I couldn't instantly turn all that off.

My first step was to accept situations as they were and stop pouring emotions into the outcomes. My new mentors shared an Old Taoist story with me that helped me to understand this idea.

One day in late summer, an old farmer was working in his field with his old, sick horse. The farmer decided to let his horse loose to go to the mountains and live out the rest of its life. The neighbors from the nearby village visited, offering their condolences, and said, "What a shame. Now your only horse is gone. How unfortunate you are! You must be very sad. How will you live, work the land, and prosper?" The farmer replied, "Who knows? We shall see."

Two days later, the old horse came back with twelve younger, healthier horses that followed the old horse into the corral. The villagers said, "How fortunate you are! You must be very happy!" Again, the farmer said, "Who knows? We shall see."

The story goes on with the farmer's son breaking his leg trying to train one of the wild horses. The villagers thought that was bad because the son couldn't help on the farm. But, because of the broken leg, he wasn't called to fight in the army, which of course they said was good. The son ended up with a limp, but in the end, the other young village boys all died in the war. The old farmer and his son were the only men capable of working the village lands and became wealthy. The villagers said this was great, but of course, the farmer said, "Who knows? We shall see!"

The moral of the story is to not put judgement on the situation and label it good or bad. My mentors taught me to plan the plans and not the outcomes. It's okay to make plans in my life; I have control over that. But I don't have control over the outcomes, so I need to accept them as they are and make adjustments from there. Learning and living this concept freed up my mind from value judgements so I could start approaching life with an attitude of gratitude.

The path my life took in 2009 is a great example of this. I had a sales job at an internet company, making good money, and I was very happy. Then I got fired.

Everyone said, "That's horrible."

I said, "I don't know if it's horrible."

Then I get another job right away at a start-up company.

Everyone said, "That's great." I said, "I don't know if it's great."

Then all those guys smoked pot, and I decided to leave.

Everyone said, "That's horrible."

I said, "I don't know if it's horrible."

Turns out it wasn't. Had I not gotten fired by the Internet company, then hired by the potheads and left that job, I wouldn't have considered as seriously doing my own thing. I may never have started MenuTrinfo® if none of that had happened. So, I am grateful for how it all worked out.

This perspective of coming at life from an attitude of gratitude is more than saying my glass is half full or my glass is half empty, it's saying, "Wow, I have a glass!" It was like with each job my glass was filled up, then when the job was gone, it was empty again. But I still had the glass, so before I started my company, I had the choice to fill it with another job or take control and venture out on my own. I was grateful to have that option.

This viewpoint also allowed me to pivot the company and start to offer allergy training along with menu labeling. Had I freaked out when the menu label law was pushed back another year and looked at it as a terrible misfortune, I wouldn't have a million-dollar company now. I had to take a step back, appreciate what I did have, and work with that. An attitude of gratitude doesn't stop challenges from happening, but it does make them easier to handle.

This attitude works when I am dealing with my employees as well. As CEO, there have been many times when employees walk in my office, shut the door, and by the look on their faces, it is not good news. They share a mistake, a problem they can't solve, or something about another employee they feel I should know. I doubt business school teaches students to look at all things through eyes of gratitude, but it's what I do.

I don't judge the employees for opening up to me. I see the shortcoming or mistake as a blessing because:

They trusted me enough to tell me the truth.

They respected me enough to know I will take care of it if I can.

They appreciate the company enough that they want to see it keep going.

For me, focusing on the mistake doesn't help the situation. I choose to see what good can come from it and how we can all learn and do better next time.

Help and Thank you

I ditched faith when I was about 13. The childhood God I learned about in Sunday school left me when I got abused as a kid. In my mind, no God would let a little girl be hurt that way. The end of the abuse happened when I was around the same age I lost all faith.

In my early 20s, when I decided to change my life, I needed to believe in a spiritual power outside of myself. Whether that be God, Buddha, the moon, the stars, whatever, I knew I didn't have the strength to stop drinking on my own. I needed something stronger to enable me to live a life to be proud of. When I took alcohol out of my life, I had to find a sufficient substitute.

I drank to cover up a God-Shaped hole in my soul. I poured alcohol into it with the hope it would fill it up and complete me. I needed a spiritual solution to stop drinking and fill that empty space. The problem with getting sober isn't putting the bottle of wine down for one day, it is keeping it down day in and day out. Without a higher power, without a belief in something outside myself, I couldn't do it.

I call this time my spiritual kindergarten. My childhood God had left my brain, so I needed something else.

My mentor said, "You need to pray."

"But I don't know how to pray," I said. "And I don't know who or what to pray to."

"All you need to know about God is that you are not Him," she said. "Just talk to Him. Because without a higher power, you are not going to stay sober, and wine will continue to be the answer."

Wrapping my mind around this idea of some higher power outside of me that I couldn't see challenged me. I needed something physical, something concrete. A yellow stuffed dog became the solution to my problem, giving me that visual I needed.

My daily practice became prayers of "help" and "thanks" to the stuffed animal. I asked for help in the morning to get up and make the right choices, do the right thing, be the right kind of Betsy who has a real job, is responsible, and acts like an adult. Then at night it was thanks that I made it through the day, there was nothing to regret, and nothing I needed to go apologize to someone for.

After about four months into my sobriety, I became incredibly sick with an infection. I went to the hospital, my higher power stuffed dog under my arm, and ended up being admitted for seven days of IV antibiotics.

While in the hospital, I experienced an incredible outpouring of love and support from my new friends and non-drinking community. Every day people came to visit. The phone in my room rang so much, I had to unplug it sometimes in order to get rest. I saw God working through these people.

One phone call was from someone I didn't even know. "I just heard you were in the hospital and that you are new to us. I want you to know that I am praying for you. If there is anything you need, let me know. I drive by that hospital every day."

People would come before work, after work. They'd bring dinner and hang out. The support blew my mind and overwhelmed me with emotion. I had never experienced anything like it before. It was an outward example of God showing up and letting me know I was not alone.

On day six, the doctor told me they would to need to do laparoscopic surgery to remove the rest of the infection and that could mean losing my ovaries and fallopian tubes. That night I looked at my stuffed dog and said, "I don't know what is going to happen tomorrow, but it is in your hands. Whatever will be, will be." I closed my eyes, took a deep breath, and a sense of peace filled my body, allowing me to let go and trust.

The next morning after surgery, a friend was waiting for me. I asked him, "What did they have to take out?"

"Nothing."

"What do you mean nothing?" I asked.

"Betsy, they didn't take anything."

"You've got to be kidding."

"No, I'm not."

I met with the doctor, and he said, "I don't have an explanation for this. You have your tubes, your ovaries. In my mind, I didn't think you come out with everything, but you did."

"Maybe there is a God," I thought.

When I got home the next day, I took my higher power stuffed dog and placed him on a shelf. I thanked him but told him I didn't need him anymore. I was beginning to understand there might be something out there.

I continued my prayers without my yellow friend. My spiritual shift wasn't because of one earth shattering incident. It has been a slow water drip over the years. My time in the hospital showed me I wasn't alone. When I was paralyzed with fear and hid under the bed until my friend came to get me, I was shown I could trust. I watched people who talked about having a higher power, then walked as if they did. Or saw those who said they believed in being of service to others and then showed that with their actions. All of this began to fill that spiritual hole inside of me. When a friend took me to the pharmacy to get medication for a virus, or when a stranger showed up at my door to take me to get a car, that was God showing up.

With every incident, my eyes and heart opened wider, and I paid more attention to my surroundings. Something would come across my path, and I just knew it was God. Whether it was a butterfly, a job offer, or a friendship, I could tell it was a message. I started to give credit to a higher spirit and realized something outside of me was helping and being my coach.

This sense that I was not alone provided me with incredible strength and hope. It got me through those challenging early years of staying sober and opened my eyes to the amazing world around me.

Facebook

Facebook has been influential throughout my story. It is how I got the idea for the business. It is how I share with others, and how I stay connected. A few years ago, my lungs started to get worse because I wasn't on the intense chemo anymore. Scleroderma has never left in all these years, but it's changed its face. It went from my hard skin to softer skin, and then it went to my insides, affecting my lungs. Then eventually my heart.

It was not an easy time. I needed to flip the script and change my perspective on the situation. It was time to stop thinking that life was an endurance contest and remember the good things. My lungs weren't perfect, but at least I could still breathe. There were people in the world who didn't have two lungs; there were people who didn't have two working legs. I had to shift my outlook and get back to being grateful for the little stuff, like breath, as well as the big stuff, like my company breaking the million-dollar mark.

I turned to Facebook and used it as a forum to count my blessings. Every morning, following my prayer and meditation time, I paused to think about the blessings in my life, and then I would share one online. I put the date, the word *Gratitude,* and one sentence. My focus was that of gratitude and not one of lack, dysfunction, depression, sadness, or I'm in trouble.

It made an incredible difference in my life. Even if I woke up and thought *Holy hell, how am I going to get through today? I can't breathe well. It's cold, and it hurts.* Taking the time to do this colored the whole day in a positive light, even if I didn't totally feel it. I did this for an entire year.

I chose this forum because it is part of me living out loud. Plus, doing it publicly held me accountable. If I skipped a day, someone would ask where my post was. Or I would get private messages from someone saying, "Do you know how much I depend on reading your post every morning?" There were times I struggled to come up with something, so I would say, "I've got nothing today. What are you all grateful for?" I'd get dozens of comments from people sharing their blessings, and this lifted my spirits. The positive love I got back during that year was unreal. These simple daily thoughts reached out and touched others; they were of service to them as much as they were a service to me.

Almost There

Coming from a place of gratitude has helped me cope with my scleroderma. Back in chapter one, I mentioned the new doctor who asked if he could hit me with a bus in order to treat my disease. As part of the whole *bus* plan, he started me on new treatment of Methotrexate. It is a cancer drug from 1957 that is an immune system suppressant. It would stop my immune system, and as a result, cause the disease to stop attacking me. It put scleroderma in a time out. There is no cure, but while I took this poison, it prevented the disease from progressing.

My stomach is rock solid, so it can handle lots of drugs. It worked against me when I was drinking and drugging because I could keep going long after I should have stopped, but here it worked in my favor. Not everyone can take Methotrexate because of what it does to your body, like my friend I met through my scleroderma group. We were both diagnosed at the same time with the same type of scleroderma. She couldn't take this drug, and she passed away nine years ago.

The biggest challenge with this medication was it compromised my immune system. My body could not fight a common cold or stomach bug. If someone was sick around me, and I caught it, it would hit me like a ton of bricks. The medication also caused me to lose most of my hair, and I had to get my liver and kidneys checked each month.

When I first began taking the drug, the doctor told me it would take about six months for it to kick in, and then anywhere from a year to 18 months to take full effect. Instead of focusing on the side effects, I shifted my focus and did daily gratitude lists. Regardless of how horrible I felt, or the amount of pain I was experiencing, I made a point to find something to appreciate each day, even when the doctor kept extending the amount of time he wanted me on the drug. It ended up being 2½ years.

After 53 weeks of treatment, I told Rocky, "I'm almost done!"

He looked at me like I was crazy, "Bets, you still have 51 weeks to go."

"I know," I said. "But, I'm on the downside. I can see the finish line. It's easier for me to think this is more than halfway over, than to think I still have 51 weeks to go."

He chuckled and said, "I can see your point."

After 2 ½ years of this daily, nasty treatment, I was finally able to stop the medication. With scleroderma, there's a test you give yourself called a skin score. This is where you pinch your skin together to see if you can grab any loose skin. Before I started the Methotrexate, my skin was like trying to pinch together the top of a table, but during the treatment, it started to soften, and by the time the treatment was over, I had the use of my hands back. My husband didn't have to dress me anymore. The methotrexate worked!

Keeping the focus on the positive and celebrating the halfway point helped keep me in the right mindset through the long treatment. Making that shift from *Oh no, I still have 51 weeks,* to *I am almost there,* made a world of difference. I use this in the office with my employees too. When they are working hard on a project, under a tight deadline, and we get to that midpoint, I will tell them they are in the homestretch and almost there. Its sets an encouraging tone, making it easier to push through to the finish.

Passing It On

I belong to a private Facebook page, Dining Out With Food Allergies, that has over 18 thousand followers. A food allergy mom jumped onto the page to share a great experience she had at a popular Chinese food chain. I thought this restaurant should know how grateful this mom felt for such a positive experience dining out with her child there. With her permission, I copied what she wrote and sent it on to the head of food safety for that restaurant chain saying, "This is the impact you are making."

He was thrilled and so grateful I shared this with him. It allowed me to share the gratitude both ways, which was wonderful. It allowed me to be the middle person. The restaurants I work with, who share my passion for food safety, put a lot of time and effort into making sure their food allergy customers are treated well. These restaurants need to hear when they are doing it right and that their efforts matter. If I can help facilitate that, I will.

We Love Our Clients

As a company, we value and appreciate our clients, and we express this through how we treat them. It's so much more than a one-time *Thank you for your business.* During phone calls, we let them know how much we appreciate their partnership and their trust in us to provide them with accurate information and numbers. I remind our early clients that although I started MenuTrinfo® and AllerTrain™, it was them who helped build it into the company it is today.

At the big trade show every year in Chicago, we always have a special gift just for our clients. We give out swag to anyone who stops by, but for our clients, we give them something extra. To show them they are celebrities to us, we always take our pictures with them.

For AllerTrain™, we now have Master Trainers of the month. A plaque with all their names on it hangs in our office. We send them a nice certificate for their wall and share their accomplishment all over our social media with mentions, videos, and pictures. We give out yearly food allergy awards to restaurants. The winners receive plaques for their locations, and we send out press releases to let the world know what a difference they are making in the lives of many.

What I Give Back, I Get

I believe what I give out, I get back. With my business, I am so grateful about what my company gets to do. We aren't just selling widgets, we are protecting lives and health through nutrition and training. Our trainings and nutrition information help people of all ages stay healthy and not experience reactions from allergens. I had a mommy blogger reach out to me because her daughter's school was not taking the right precautions to keep the girl safe from allergens, and it nearly killed her. I told her, of course I would help. The next day I called the school and asked them to pick the days and times they wanted training. I informed them I would send someone in person to do the training, or do it remotely, at no cost to the school.

I have given away classes, workbooks, posters, and Aller-Cards, maybe 100 times now in the last four years. This is where my gratitude for getting to do what I do shows up, and I can help others.

On a personal level, for the past year and a half since my parents both passed away, I have been looking at older people differently and paying more attention to them.

Recently, I sat next to an old gentleman on a plane. We started talking, and this sweet man told me about his time in serving in Vietnam as well as his job as a DEA agent and an FBI agent. I enjoyed the hell out of him. When the plane landed, I felt compelled to help him get safely to his son waiting for him in baggage claim. Together we got off the plane. I joked with him the whole way as he shuffled along with his cane while I carried his oxygen machine. Before turning him over to his son, I gave my new friend a big hug and kiss on the cheek. I had even called Rocky to come in, instead of just picking me up outside, so he could meet him too.

I felt grateful I got to enjoy that man's company. Had I stayed in my own little bubble, I never would have noticed.

Earlier this week during a bitter cold snap, I saw an elderly woman with one crutch trying to cross the icy street to her house. I pulled over and got out of my warm car to help her. As we crossed the street, she told me, "You are an absolute sweetheart." I told her I really wasn't, but I was glad I could be of service. After getting her safely in her house, I went back in my car to thaw out. The woman didn't know my name, I didn't know her, yet I had a positive impact on her day.

Maybe people who grow up in normal families do this stuff every day, I didn't. I was never shown how to give without expecting. But these simple acts of service fill me with gratitude because I can help someone. It's like walking my spirituality. I can say I am a spiritual person filled with gratitude, but if I don't act on it, then I am not. Throughout my life, I have been able to be of service to those I knew, but this recent shift has me extending that to strangers. It now goes beyond giving back without any expectation because these people don't have an option to "pay me back." That old man won't be able to find me again. The women I helped across the street doesn't even know my name. I don't think God has a scorecard that says since you helped that old lady, I am going to make your business successful. But I think if I don't help that old lady, then I stay self-centered and miss out on the beauty and opportunities around me.

My world is full and abundant. Taking the time to stop and appreciate the good things around me keeps me open and ready for more blessings to flow my direction. Stepping out to be of service to others is a way for me to outwardly express my gratitude and continue walking my spiritual path. But gratitude is more than just an action or something I share on Facebook, it is part of who I am, deep in my core, and reminds me every new day is a blessing.

Gratitude: Food for Thought

➤ Starting out with prayer and/or meditation can set the tone for the day. Regardless of your religious beliefs, taking 10 minutes each morning to get quiet and pray or calm all the thoughts racing through your mind can make a world of difference. Commit to doing this for two weeks, then reflect on how it is affecting your life.

➤ In this chapter, I talk about my one year of posting a daily gratitude on Facebook. I encourage you to try this for 30 days. It doesn't have to be on social media. It can be in a journal, but each day, write down (or post) one thing you are grateful for. After the 30 days, reflect on the impact this exercise may or may not have had on your attitude.

➤ Clients and customers are essential to most businesses. What do you do to make them feel appreciated? If this is an area you need to improve in, what are three ways you can show your appreciation? Pick one of those to do right away.

➤ Giving back without expecting anything in return is an important element of gratitude. In what ways do you give back at work? In your personal life? Do you need to improve in this area? If so, what are three ways you can do this.

CHAPTER 12

Complete Recipe

suc·cess (noun) the accomplishment of an aim or purpose.

Throughout this book, I shared ten spiritual principles that guided me from my 20s until now. They laid a foundation for me as I pushed through alcoholism and drug abuse, gave me hope when I thought I was going to die, and provided me the tools I needed to create a thriving, million-dollar company.

These ten ingredients are the staples for a strong recipe to accomplish success in life and in business. They will act as a guide, directing your decisions and actions as you navigate challenges and triumphs just as they have done mine.

Write them down and post them somewhere to keep them in the front of your mind. Might I suggest sticky notes on your bathroom mirror changing out the principle weekly. Or in your car or one of my personal favorites, use them as rotating passwords for logging into your computer or a specific program you might touch multiple times a day like email. The repetition helps reaffirm the movement towards this way of looking at the world. You have to log in why not use a mundane task like that for good and growth?

1. Passion
2. Integrity
3. Self-Support
4. Ask for Help
5. Persistence
6. Courage
7. Wisdom
8. Honesty
9. Unity
10. Gratitude

When your life feels overwhelming and stressful, or you feel lost possibly out of control, think about these principles and ask yourself these questions:

Passion: Do I have passion for what I am doing?

Integrity: Am I approaching people and situations with integrity?

Self-Support: Am I relying too much on other people?

Ask for Help: Am I trying to shoulder all of the burdens?

Persistence: Do I need to continue investing time and energy into a situation, or do I need to re-evaluate?

Courage: How do I find the strength and courage to make it through my current circumstances?

Wisdom: What areas of my life could use more education to gather wisdom either through formal schooling a mentor or another means?

Honesty: Am I being completely honest with both myself and those I work with in how I am conducting business?

Unity: Do I view other businesses as competition and shy away from partnering with them because I am afraid they will take business away from me?

Gratitude: Am I viewing my life through the lens of gratefulness?

Monthly Focus

To really embrace this idea of living your life with these principles as the foundation, try this over the next ten months. Look at the list and rank them in order, from 1 to 10, with the one you feel is most lacking in your life at number one and the one you are strongest with at ten.

Starting at the top of your list, choose one principle to focus on each month. Re-read that chapter of the book, then pay attention to times when you are using it or when you should have been using it but didn't. Even though you are focusing more attention on one specific principle, don't disregard the rest.

To hit the point home, get a notebook, and each morning or evening jot down a couple of sentences about how that principle played out in your life. If you are not much for writing, then find a friend who will do this with you. Touch base with each other once a week over coffee or the phone and share your thoughts, reflections, and revelations. Whether you are journaling on your own or sharing with a friend, you can use the questions at the end of each chapter to guide you.

You Got This!

Life can be messy. Sometimes we make bad choices which can lead to challenges. Other times, like with Scleroderma, things happen to us that are out of our control. Regardless of how we got there, we have to be able to navigate through the undesirable circumstances. By adhering to these principles in all that you do, you will have the tools needed to happier, less stressed, and able to work through situations easier. The problems won't disappear, but you will be able to cope better.

As you move forward in your journey, know that you rock, and you have what it takes to live a fulfilling and happy life. By following my recipe for success, I believe you will be well on your way to being unstoppable!

Acknowledgments

First and foremost, there is not a single word that can be written without the support, love, and patience of my family. Rocky, my dear sweet husband you are my partner in all things and my rock in life. I love you to my core and thank you for all you do and have done to get us to today. Victoria Grace, you are my greatest blessing and my biggest teacher. You have allowed me to have the very best job of my entire life, your mom. Raising a daughter and watching you become the strong, smart, kind and wonderful young lady you have become is by far my best I have to give and leave to the world. To my step sons, both Jeff and John, you have both taught me a great deal about what unconditional love looks like and for those lessons I thank both of you. To my former husbands, both Dennis and Steve. Thank you for the parts and roles you have played along the way. I respect and appreciate both of you and am so grateful to call both of you great men my friends today. To my Brother, JD thanks for lighting the way to anything is possible like writing a book, giving a talk and raising above. And finally, to my Sister in law, Sara you amaze me with your brilliance and kindness. I aspire to be more like you in many ways.

To my employees that helped and continue to build MenuTrinfo® with me. You are and have all been pieces of this beautiful mission. The ones that came and left and the ones that stayed. We would not be where we are without each and every single one of you. I hope wherever you are today you are successful, happy and strong in your passion. Thank you for being strong in mine to assist and grow it with me.

In business I have met so many brilliant, amazing, leaders along my way to these words in this book. It is hard to name all and not forget some, however there are a few that I simply must acknowledge here. Kathleen, Marla, Sue, Todd, Burt, Alicia, Bill, Dr. John, Mike, Kristi, Allison, Greg, Chet, Chase, Cam, William, Carin, Jim, Hal, Paul, Michele, Kerrie, and all the clients who have become friends, mentors and guides I thank you and everyone for the contributions you have made to my mission and life.

Finally, a heartfelt thank you to those that have sponsored me and been amazing mentors along the way and those I have been gifted to sponsor and mentor. Too many to name but you know who you are and your fingerprints rest on my heart. Thank you.

ABOUT THE AUTHOR

Award-winner Betsy Craig is the CEO and founder of Menu-Trinfo®, LLC, AllerTrain™ by MenuTrinfo, Kitchens with Confidence, and Food Handlers. She is the national leading expert on food safety, saving people's lives, and health through nutrition and training.

Throughout her 10+-year trailblazing career in food safety, Betsy has been interviewed by national publications such as The Wall Street Journal, The Boston Globe, The New York Times, and Food Safety Magazine. She spoke before an FDA/USDA panel in 2017, and has presented at industry-related events, including the National Restaurant Association, multiple International Food Technologist Conferences, the New York, California, and Florida State Restaurant & Foodservice Shows, Pizza Expo, and the FARE College and University Conference. Betsy has been a guest speaker at over 100 shows, expos, educational sessions, and brand conferences to date.

Betsy founded—MenuTrinfo, LLC® offering AllerTrain™, Kitchens with Confidence™, and the newest offering, a

202 • BETSY CRAIG

National Food Handlers course— these provide a complete suite of services that includes menu labeling and nutritional analysis, food allergies and food sensitivities certification and training, kitchen audits for food service, and certification for allergen and gluten free products. AllerTrain™ was the first ANSI accredited food allergy and only gluten-free training class in the food service industry.

In addition to being named the Bravo 2013 Emerging Entrepreneur of the Year, Betsy's professional and business awards include being named a 2012 and 2013 Fast Casual Top Mover & Shaker, 2015 Northern Colorado Super Women award, and 2015/2016 Mercury Top 100 Northern Colorado business awards.

www.BetsyCraig.com

CPSIA information can be obtained
at www.ICGtesting.com
Printed in the USA
FFOW01n1250200518
46749408-48921FF